ONE WAY OUT

ONE WAY OUT

The Story of a Baby Boomer
Chasing His American Dream

Jim Azzarelli

iUniverse, Inc.
New York   Bloomington

iUniverse books may be ordered through booksellers or by contacting:

iUniverse
1663 Liberty Drive
Bloomington, IN 47403
www.iuniverse.com
1-800-Authors (1-800-288-4677)

ISBN: 978-1-4401-2786-1 (pbk)
ISBN: 978-1-4401-2787-8 (ebk)

Printed in the United States of America

iUniverse rev. date: 7/7/2009

Acknowledgments

I'd like to first thank my parents, Sam and Jean Azzarelli, who nourished me and raised me in tumultuous times, through the great generation gap of the 1960s and '70s. I'd like to thank my brothers and sisters, Ray, Rick, Paula, Mary, Jeanne, and Greg, for providing support as a family unit, being there with some laughs in the crazy days of our youth and up until the present. I give special appreciation to my wife, Mary, who has always taken me for who I am, with all my warts, hang-ups, baggage, and craziness. Through it all you've cared for me, and I am eternally grateful that we have shared this window of eternity together. Without you, this book would never have been written. Also thanks to my children, Jill, Amy, Jay, and Andrew, for giving my life a true purpose and a big reason to always push forward.

Contents

INTRODUCTION

One Way Out is about the path that I chose, but we are all choosing a path whether we know it or not. Whether we like it or not, we are moving. Life is constantly moving. We move out of our house, move out of our neighborhood, move out of our job, move out of a relationship, and eventually, move out of our bodies and this life. The only constant is change. It's how we deal with those changes that winds up making a difference in our lives.

My grandfather, Raymond Azzarelli, saw one way out of his situation in the old country. He moved out of Sicily in 1906 and forged a new life in a new world. He moved out of this existence after ninety-three hard-fought years of a good life lived. He rarely had it easy. Not until his later years did the family achieve a modicum of success, but even then he grinded and worked hard in his garden both in Illinois and in Florida. Work was his happiness, and his sons brought him joy through an undying respect and willingness to work together to create a family bond that would branch out through generations to come. His way out of poverty was to come to the United States, and I will be eternally grateful that he did.

My way out was to move away from the company that the family started after World War II because of conditions I found to be unacceptable for my future growth as a person and businessman. My way out took me to Florida, my dream destination from childhood. After some years of working in one of the family businesses there, my next way out was to start my own enterprise. I had varying degrees of success, and in 2003 I hit a low point in my professional life. I considered my options to get out of my misery, until I picked up a book and saw the one way out. The book was the Bible, and it gave me an answer that I saw as the way out.

I wrote this book not as just a biography of one baby boomer's sojourn through the middle and latter stages of the twentieth century and into the new millennium, but hopefully as an inspiration to all who struggle with the everyday decisions that weigh upon us all. Most decisions are small ones that amount to small consequences, but every so often, a big choice comes along and we must be willing to step into the great unknown or take the so-called leap of faith forward to the next phase of life. In the book I call these windows of opportunity. We must be willing to climb through those windows to get what we want, or at least what we think we want, and pray that the consequences are indeed what we intended.

I hope you enjoy this writing, and remember: keep moving forward, but always consider the past.

CHAPTER ONE
The Dream

For most of my life, I have been trying to break out of a slavery of sorts. While this slavery is not really anyone's fault, it is just as real, in its own way, as the yoke over the Jews during their slavery in Egypt. Birthed out of a particular set of circumstances that is not uncommon in modern America, my slavery is self-induced, I suppose. We may be free and we even may be living the American Dream, but we often are not happy. We do not feel we can allow ourselves to be happy. Our baby boomer generation is so completely different than the previous one that we often have felt that we are on our own. Growing up, I received very little help on how to channel my creative dreams for my life. Saying such things releases major guilt trips in all of us, but it is best understood in the microcosm of our rather large family—my dad and mom, three brothers, three sisters, and me in the middle.

I've always had big dreams. I knew I could accomplish great things. But as the Bible says, "the sprit is willing, but the flesh is weak." I often felt like something was holding me back. I knew I could soar above it somehow. This became my mission.

Not a lot of great karma has been passed down through the Sicilian heritage. Here was a group of people who were so impoverished and abandoned by the separated mainland of Italy that the only real government that emerged was the Mafia. We all know the mob was bad news, but my dad always said that *Mafia* in Italian just means "my family." Amazing, isn't it? It's a family thing! Well, the Sicilian people were so impoverished that they took to bullying, killing, stealing, or whatever was necessary to take care of their families. The mob pretty much became the government for the island, and they decided to emigrate to New York and beyond. I'm not here to write about gangsters, but it is a big part of the Sicilian heritage. The mob was in the construction business in northern Illinois and I could never escape the questions such as, "How can you be sure your family isn't in La Cosa Nostra?" That was a good question given our close proximity to Chicago, the home of Al Capone and Bugs Moran. My response was always that I never saw any strange black limos, hit men with black shirts and white ties, or FBI agents sniffing around our little slice of paradise on the lovely plains of northern Illinois. I sort of liked the idea that people thought we were in the mob, but it scared me at the same time. I fantasized about us being in control of all the business deals and the power that came with the aura of being a mobster.

Our little city of Kankakee didn't have the mob. But when it came to the construction business, we pretty much controlled our town, just as the mob controlled Chicago. Kankakee is connected to two other small towns, Bradley and Bourbonnais, with a total population of about 80,000. Being sixty miles south of Chicago made us pretty much a forgotten burgh, but as I grew up, I saw our little company grow into a powerhouse of a construction enterprise. I lived by the main highway, Highway 17, where I'd play in my sandbox with my trucks watching the big trucks—dump trucks, concrete trucks, and lowboy trucks— roll down the road to their project destinations, building the company that would grow and eventually branch out to Tampa, my future home and the home of my children.

I used to stand by the road hoping that one of the trucks would stop, pick me up, and take me around to the jobs. Of course they never did. I was probably five at the time, and I loved the smell of the trucks, the diesel fuel, the dirt—it was in my blood. Something happened to crystallize these feelings in me when I went to kindergarten. I attended St. Stan's in town and felt like I'd made it to the big time when a company dump truck would pick me up after school to take me home. Red Rinnish drove the truck and treated me like a king. The kids would marvel at me and be jealous because they had to ride home with their mom or grandpa. How drab! I had a chauffer and a dump truck at my disposal to take me home. So it was that my destiny was ordained. I loved the construction business from the time I was five.

Humble Beginnings

Nanu, my grandpa, emigrated from in Sicily in 1906, part of the largest mass exodus from the country—several million Italians escaping the boot and especially the island where droughts, earthquakes and floods were the norm. Hitting New York at the prime age of nineteen, Nanu was recruited immediately to do dirty and dangerous work on the New York Central Railroad. About one hundred Italian immigrants were killed during its construction. Later, Nanu worked at a quarry, loading rail cars by shovel, working back-to-back twelve-hour shifts. They would rest one twelve-hour shift after working two. In those days, twelve hours of hard work brought in about $1.25, but coming from his meager surroundings in Pozzolo, Sicily, he took what he could get. He eventually made his way to Chicago to work for the railroad, then to Thawville, a tiny community south of Kankakee. He then returned to Sicily for Nana, his bride, and brought her back to America with him. These were brutal times—leaving your family and knowing you may never see them again in the hopes of starting a better life.

Eventually, Nanu and Nana came to Kankakee and began their slow climb up the ladder of society. At first they lived in two box cars hooked together in a west Kankakee rail yard. Nanu cut a deal with the Illinois Central Railroad to maintain their right of way in exchange for the right to grow his vegetables on about ten acres along the line. Nanu knew how to wheel and deal and that meant something in America. He handed down this skill through the generations, which enabled our family to build their empire. He made his boys, Bart and Sam, get a little red wagon. It was the first piece of equipment in the empire. They went door-to-door peddling vegetables over an area about two square miles. They hated it, but later realized what a valuable lesson they had learned. Besides raising the vegetables, Nanu always held down two jobs, while Nana picked the crop for the daily run around the neighborhood. They had a chicken and a cow to provide eggs and milk to supplement the meager earnings they picked up on the route. Before long, Nanu had scraped together enough cash to buy a modest truck to haul the vegetables to markets in Kankakee and eventually to Chicago, which was a three-hour drive at the time (now it's about an hour). Nanu once took a load of beets to the major market in Chicago on Randolph Street, and someone offered him two and a half cents a bunch right away, but Nanu turned down the offer. He wanted to see if he could get more. At the end of the day, everyone was leaving and he ended up settling for a half cent per bunch. He earned $15 for two days of work. Nanu and the boys could have cried over that one. Later, I also would learn how one can sometimes get screwed in the market by adding that little extra to a bid only to lose it to a rival. It's a valuable lesson to learn, whether it costs you $15 or $150,000.

These were really challenging times for the struggling young family, and it wasn't just about making a living. Often, they would receive a black death envelope conveying the news that a loved one had passed away in the homeland. At those times there would be great longing to go back—something many immigrants did—but Nanu always refused. He and Nana had a vision, one of a better life in America for him and his family. He had the true American Dream.

Chapter Two

Growing Up on Spaghetti Hill

As the Azzarelli family began to assimilate into American society, they realized this wasn't going to be easy. America was the land of opportunity, but making good on that opportunity required a lot of hard work, and there were many obstacles to overcome. One of those was prejudice. There was plenty of anti-Italian sentiment to go around, and Italian-Americans were the butt of the dago jokes and jabs. Once, when Sam (my dad) and Bart (my uncle) were at their grade school, Nanu happened to drive by and saw them eating their lunch outside on the curb. He asked what they were doing, and they told him the teacher sent them out there and that they couldn't eat with other kids. So Nanu went inside and made the teacher an offer she couldn't refuse. It didn't happen again. When they were kids, Bart was the tough guy, beating up the guys who picked on Pete or Sam at school and making sure nobody played them for fools.

Living in town, Nanu was able to raise enough vegetables to feed the family and sell some to have a small business, but he wanted to spread his wings out in the country so he looked west of town in an area called Limestone Township. He acquired a forty-acre tract sometime before the war that eventually became our little slice of paradise and the future home of a construction powerhouse. He thought it would be a good place to grow produce, but it proved to be too sandy. So he just held on to the land and looked at it as a long-term investment. His friends use to joke that the property was only good for "raising kids and sandburs." But little did they know that this mountain of sand proved to be the perfect place to grow a construction empire. Sand is the gold of the construction business. If you own sand, you control the jobs, because all the jobs need fill delivered to build the foundation for the building or to fill low areas of the job site. Having this sand gave my family an advantage over the competition. Nanu's land had plenty of sand, including a sixty-foot sand hill that was two hundred feet wide. Those forty acres housed all the necessary ingredients for our construction empire. It had a main office, the home of the central power brokers: Nanu, my uncles, and my father. It had the shop where the equipment was maintained and repaired, several sheds where various tools and other equipment were stored, and plenty of other room to store the dump trucks and heavy-duty road equipment.

Our little slice of paradise had a swimming pool (built by the construction company), which was unheard of at that time, with a park complete with a basketball court. I spent countless hours there honing my limited basketball skills, dreaming of being a college basketball star, which I knew would probably never happen. I was too short and too white. We had a large corn field in the back of the subdivision, and the sand hill stood at the rear of the field. That was our winter playground. We would wax down our saucers and fly down that hill as fast as possible. We would light fires and cook hot dogs even in the wintertime. I loved that sand hill and so did Nanu. Eventually the sand hill had to be leveled and hauled away for projects. I couldn't understand it at the time, but it had to go. It was a sign of progress, my family said. It was the first time I began to see that the only constant is change. As much as I loved that hill and our paradise, I hated the cold and the dark desolation of the Illinois winters. As lovely as the springs and summers were, the cold winter winds would come, and so would my dark depression of knowing how many days, weeks, and months I had to endure until the green grass and sweet smell of leather gloves and baseballs would return.

We even had our own baseball field right behind our house, complete with a backstop and Uncle Johnnie's fence and Nanu's snow fence serving as the home run fence. All the neighborhood kids came to our park to play ball, go swimming, and play basketball. We were the power brokers of the neighborhood. It was the idyllic place to grow up; Norman Rockwell couldn't have painted a better picture. Our subdivision, which we developed, had streets named after all of my aunts and Nana. Still today you can drive down Jean Street (my mom), Betty Lane (aunt), Vivian Street (aunt), Barbara Street (aunt), and Raymond Drive (Nanu). It was our little kingdom, the little place we called Hillside Manor. In the early years, before the families began to move to other locals, the "hill," which was really just a rise in the corn field, was called "Spaghetti Hill" because there were so many Sicilians living there together. There was brother Pete, Raymond, the patriarch, Sam, my dad, and brother Bart Azzarelli, along with Frank (brother-in-law) and Josephine Raspolich, the sister in the family.

Joe Azzarelli, the eventual power broker of the empire, never did live on Spaghetti Hill. He was always the independent one, always calling his own shots. I always admired Joe. He once gave me a book, *The Power of Positive Thinking*. I read it several times and purchased the audio version later. It influenced my life immensely. Little gestures, such as giving a book to someone, can have larger implications than one could ever imagine.

During the Spaghetti Hill years, the family was about as tight as they would ever be. It was the formative years of the great Azzarelli Construction Company. The first and foremost basis of construction is hard work. That is one area these guys never shied away from as they grew up dirt poor during the grueling years of the Great Depression. These were the early days of a company that would explode and become one of the major players in the construction scene in central Illinois for the last half of the twentieth century.

But first came Pearl Harbor, D-day (in which my father participated), the Battle of the Bulge, and ultimately Hiroshima and Nagasaki. Pete became a Marine, and Sam and Bart were in the army. It was reported that Bart walked and hitchhiked two hundred miles just to see Sam when they were both in Germany. Joe trained pilots at a naval center, and Johnnie joined the army but never was sent overseas because of deafness in one ear. He served two years and received an honorable discharge. Then he went back to school and became the only one of the six siblings to have graduated from high school. It is well understood that Nana and her rosary prayed those boys back from the war. While in Italy, my father had been assigned a jeep. In camp, a sergeant told him to go to town for provisions. When he returned there was a large bomb shell hole where his jeep had been parked. I think Nana was saying the rosary at that moment. It was always her prayer that she would see her boys again, and she did. Thank God for Nana!

The Catholic religion has always been a huge part of our family life. I always went along with the religion, going to Catholic kindergarten, grade school, and high school, but never really took it to heart until later in life, especially when my own business was sinking into oblivion.

During the war, Nanu worked as driver at Florence Stove, which made shells for the government. He worked two trucks at a time because drivers were so scarce. On his trips to Chicago, Nana would buy vegetables and bring them back to

Kankakee to sell them at their new stand at the rear of the house he built in West Kankakee, across from the Stove company. The house was only half of a house and a full basement. It was all they could afford at the time, but compared to the two box cars it was like a mansion. Later, the house became a large, two-story house that my dad was always proud to show his kids as we drove by on our way to town.

After the war the boys held various jobs. Sam and Bart worked for Florence Stove as well. It was the big factory in town. Joe was working in Chicago as a corporate pilot, but work got slow and he became a customer rep for a manufacturing outfit. He got transferred to New York, but he didn't like it, so he went to Michigan and finally returned to Kankakee to be with the family.

Pete borrowed some cash from Nanu and started an excavating company with Frank Raspolich. Sam and Bart owned a small semi dump truck, which they would drive after work. Pete dug the sand and delivered truckloads to home sites in West Kankakee, where Florence Stove was financing homes for the workers. Each home site needed five loads of sand. His deal was going pretty well, but Nanu saw a good future if the family could all pull together. He realized he needed Joe to commit in order for the pieces of the puzzle to fit. They finally got their act together and started the company in 1948. Nanu had a couple of trucks to go with Pete's excavator, Bart and Sam had their little semi truck, and Joe had the brains to put it all together. They bought a crawler dozier and a crane and started building the empire from there. They hit it at just the right time—the largest growth period in the history of the United States was about to take place.

At first it was anything but easy. Every business has its stumbling points when it begins. The Azzarellis started as a hauling company for one the largest contractors in Illinois, Triangle Construction Company. When Triangle canceled their contract because they wanted to lease their own trucks, it was a devastating blow. Pete went to Joe, exclaiming that they were out of business because they had just lost their main account. That's when most people would've buckled under. But not Joe Azzarelli. He didn't flinch. He calmly stated, "Well, then, we'll have to go into the contracting business ourselves."

They were going to compete against the big boys, a formidable task. One of the first bids they put out was a rather large sewer job, more than $200,000 (which at that time was gigantic for them). Usually, at the local bid openings, there was only the one main player, Triangle. Playing it cool and smart, Joe stayed outside the room until the last minute before the deadline. Hubert Loiselle, the main man for Triangle, must've thought he was sitting pretty until Joe Azzarelli walked in at the last second with a bid. Old Hubert's cigar fell out of his mouth. Azzarelli got the bid. There was a new sheriff in town, and he were here to stay. Eventually, we became larger than Triangle through nothing but hard work and maybe a little genius.

Getting a job is one thing, but doing it is quite another. One project Uncle Bart built was a small street with storm sewers at the southeast edge of town, Justine Drive. He went out to the job, nervous as could be, and went right up to the engineer on the job and explained that he didn't have a clue about what to do or steps to take to expedite the project. That takes guts! It also took some humility, but the engineer, Dick Tyson, helped him through the process. The company was cutting its teeth, but the five brothers were a quick study in the business. They were gaining momentum through the purchase of trucks and equipment and doing the work themselves. They also had to maintain the equipment, which is a large part of building a construction company. If the machinery stops, production stops, but the labor costs keep going!

Dad usually ran the ditch diggers or track hoes, Bart became efficient at laying pipe, Pete could run the road graders, and

Frank filled in other areas, such as trucking and running a caterpillar track loader, a machine which was kept as an antique on the family picnic grounds. Joe handled the administrative duties and filled in as necessary running tar trucks, one of the nastiest jobs of all, which he loved to claim that he had done frequently (but probably not). Joe took over as president for Nanu when the time came.

Later, Joe found a concrete plant in Michigan, bought it, and had it transported to town, where it still stands on West Avenue right by the railroad tracks. Frank took over that operation, which eventually split from the Azzarellis. Joe was the political arm of the company. His named appeared in the paper all the time because of the housing authority or some other deal that got our name out there. He dreamed big and told the boys to follow, and they put their boots on. There wasn't anything that could stop them. Times were definitely heady.

Chapter Three
Tampa, the Southern Empire

The migration to Tampa was not a whim. Nanu and Joe carefully planned it. Around 1938, recurring respiratory problems in the winter caused Nanu to seek the warmer climes of Florida. He became one of the original "snowbirds," a term we Floridians call those folks who come down here to live each winter, bringing their cash and growing this place like none other. In 1938, the Tampa Bay area had about 90,000 people. Today it's bursting with about 2.5 million. Nanu saw the tremendous potential Tampa—and Florida in general—had and it paid off in a big way. By 1957, it was time to spread out. Pete was a lot like his brother Joe. He was a deal maker, always looking to meet the right people and climb up in society. He was ready for Tampa, and the town was ripe for a mover and a shaker like Pete. It didn't take long. Within four years, he had the Florida division of the family company humming along, turning a profit in the budding little metropolis. By 1961, it was time to get him some help, someone who wasn't afraid to get his hands dirty, someone who knew the business of running jobs in the field. Bart was that guy, and I was devastated that Sam, my father, wasn't. I wanted to go south, but my dreams of palm trees, sunshine, and mild winters would have to be put on hold until another day.

THE 1960S

Bart got the nod to move to Tampa, and he turned out to be one of the great underground utility men in the history of the area. They still hold him in awe at the City of Tampa Department of Public Works. I think he taught them more about utilities than they could have known. He would bid work cheaply enough to get the contract, knowing that the possibility existed for conflicts and obstructions in the way of the job. When those areas were reached, he would call for a "change order," which is work that would be done at a higher percentage of profit than was originally bid. He had the city eating out of his hand because of his knowledge and understanding of sewer systems within the city. Today, it is difficult to get change orders through the city probably due to Bart. He once told me, "You've got to have a little larceny in you to compete in construction." He became the nuts and bolts icon of the Tampa leg of the empire. Bart and Pete didn't always see eye to eye. But what brothers do? The Azzarelli brothers used to fight like gangs from Italy, but Nanu was always the steadying hand, always stressing that family unity was the key to staying strong.

Tampa, in a way, was like Kankakee in that it often got overlooked. Miami, Key West, and generally the east coast of Florida were always thought of as the real Florida. The Beatles never came to Tampa but they came to Miami. (On that tour I was lucky enough to see them live at Comiskey Park in Chicago; Sam bought a bunch of us tickets for the show.) Tampa was on the left coast of Florida and generally took a back seat to Miami. It was a city of ship repairing companies, cigar factories, and, of course, the mob. Santo Traficante ruled Tampa with an iron hand from 1937 to 1945, controlling the gambling rackets in the city. I even paved the driveway of his grandson, Santo III. One time I had contact with another mobster, Frank Decidue, who was reportedly second in command behind Santo. I had just started my own fledgling company when Bart sent me down to his homestead a few miles east of downtown to give him a price to seal his driveway. I did the job not knowing who he was, but later I did see the barn where the bolita rackets were operated on the property. The state runs the lottery much the same way bolita was played back then. Organized crime operated freely, and construction wasn't a bad gig either.

Pete got involved in local politics, always trying to figure out which politician to back at election time. Usually he was right, donating funds to the winning mayoral candidate and making more connections in Tampa. Once he was going to back the incumbent, who seemed like a sure winner. He told Nanu he was thinking about donating $1,000 to his campaign, but Nanu told him to give it to the up-and-comer (he was Italian, of course) because, though everyone wanted to be on the favorite's side, if Pete donated to the underdog and he won, Pete would be a hero. The underdog won and Pete was a hero. My uncle was chosen to serve on important boards of directors, including the Tampa Port Authority and Florida Road Builders. Pete always impressed me because of his ability to slide into the right places with the right people. He also became an integral part of my own move to Florida. The brothers made important road trips to Tampa, especially in winter. (It was probably one of the great tax breaks they could've had.) They all bought beach-front condos, and we spent many Easters on the west coast of Florida.

Pete became buddies with J. W. Conner, a construction tycoon, and Jim Walters, who ran a home building empire and had a seat on the New York Stock Exchange. Sam Whitney was another cohort, a trucking magnate. I've been doing business with his son Rick for more than two decades. These men became Tampa's version of the rat pack, staying out many late nights and cutting deals over cocktails between themselves and other local businessmen. Walters had two private jets, and I was fortunate to have flown in each one on trips between Kankakee and Tampa.

In the late 1960s, Pete and J. W. were fed up with the local asphalt scene in Tampa, which was controlled almost exclusively by the Cone Brother Company. It was almost like the Triangle company up north; both J. W. and Azzarelli found it more and more difficult to get their jobs asphalted as they gained more power. Cone didn't really like them moving up the contracting ladder and made it tough to complete their projects. Around 1970, J. W. Conner & Sons, Azzarelli, and Jim Walter started Delta Asphalt Co. Walter was the cash engine behind the deal, as an asphalt plant was needed for the operation and that was a big expense. With Delta, each owner could now control his own job production and scheduling.

The Tampa operation continued to grow and prosper and Pete enjoyed his independence, away from Joe's controlling grasp. Back in Kankakee, Pete and Joe always struggled for control, but there was no question that Joe was the overall leader. In Tampa, however, Pete had a certain amount of autonomy. He was the head of his own domain and played his hand quite well in the southern leg of the empire.

The Tampa operation had its own slice of paradise on ten acres on Busch Blvd. about a mile west of Busch Gardens. Pete negotiated to purchase this property for fifty thousand dollars, a huge sum back in 1960. Then in 1969 we acquired a beach house that included five apartments through a business trade with J. W. Conner. It became know as "Azzarelli Place."

As the company grew in Florida, equipment had to be shipped from Kankakee to Tampa. The company in Illinois had surplus equipment to send south. The empire was expanding, and everyone was making money. Up north, things were moving right along as our power base within the town grew. We had two asphalt plants, three pipe crews, a bridge crew, dirt crews, concrete crews—we could build just about any type of road the city, county, or state threw at us. We were members at the local country club and were well-respected members of the community. Gone were the days of those poor little Wops from West Kankakee.

Going to Work

I started working for the company when I was about fourteen. They let me use the company riding lawn mower to tend to the company's properties, mowing them weekly, especially our baseball field. I took such great pride in that field that I tried to make it look like Comiskey Park, the home of my beloved Chicago White Sox. My dad would acquire season tickets to the Sox games, and I would go to twenty or thirty games each year. Sam was a die-hard fan, but the Sox rarely had a decent season, except for 1965, when they got hot but could manage only a second place finish. Dad was heartbroken. I think he liked taking out his frustrations on the team for not playing up to his standards. He was a successful Little League coach and took the Kankakee All-Stars to the Midwest regionals in Missouri, only to lose in the semifinals. He had to quit coaching, however, as the company grew in the sixties. He would often leave town to do sewer projects in downstate Arcola and Tuscola near Danville. He, like Bart, had a real knack for doing the sewer jobs and had a handle on the concept of drainage and the best way to achieve it.

At fifteen, I finally got my chance to work with a real crew. This was a big step, and I wanted to make the most of it, but I wound up stuck with an alcoholic foreman on road jobs in the far reaches of Kankakee County, near Indiana. I'm sure this guy didn't appreciate having "Sam's boy" on his first job. Once he sent me down this road with a power broom tractor and let me do some sweeping. I got lost, cleaning the wrong road, and got my first ass chewing. That was always a favorite saying on the crew: "He really got his ass chewed out." It was a great way to get someone's attention, and I was thoroughly embarrassed. I had a long way to go.

My next gig was on a patch crew, which I loved. I moved

from spot to spot around town, fixing potholes, flagging on the streets, and checking out the women. The great part of it was that I was outdoors and not cooped up in some office all day. There were advantages to being the boss's son, and one of them was that I sometimes could pick my own job. Most of the time I went wherever they could use an extra man on a job site.

In 1968, I was working on an alley cleanup crew near our country club when my dad drove up in his big Oldsmobile. Something was wrong; he never came to those small crews. We had heard there had been an accident earlier in the day involving my cousin, Joe Raspolich, Josephine's son. Dad called me over to the car and told me to get in. He had a nervous look about him. He simply stated, "Your cousin Joe is dead." He had been run over by an earthmover that, for whatever reason, had backed over him. Earthmovers usually make a pass to skim dirt from the ground to move it to another area. Joe was checking grade and stepped behind the machine. The operator must have felt he needed to scoop more dirt, but tragically he ran over my cousin. Joe bled to death on the way to the hospital. I couldn't believe it. As if hearing this news wasn't hard enough, I turned around to see Joe's best friend, Jeff Mackin, standing near the car. He looked at me and said, "Joe's all right, isn't he?" And I had to answer, "Joe's dead." I've never since had to tell anyone such grim news. It was devastating. This event sent shock waves throughout the family and showed how dangerous working in the field can be. Later, the Occupational Safety and Health Administration forced all trucks and heavy equipment to have backup alarms because of this accident. If the earthmover would have had one, maybe Joe would have had a chance. He was only seventeen.

Joe's death really shook my dad. He said he didn't want me working construction in the field anymore, and the next summer I spent several weeks in a trailer as a "time keeper." It was horrible. I would sit there for eight hours waiting for

3:30 to come. It was my low point of working in the business, but Dad felt that he was protecting me from the dangers of working around heavy equipment. My father was always a worrier. Everyone usually thought he was Mr. Calm and Cool, but inside he was churning with ulcers, going to job sites with a carton of milk or milk of magnesia. I think being part of the empire was a bit overwhelming to him.

A Nerve-racking Business

Construction is a nerve-racking business. First, the bid has to be put together, which on large projects can be quite tedious and time-consuming. If you are awarded the job, you are usually excited for a few days because you believe you're going to make some money. Before long, though, the tensions and concerns set in. How low were you on the bid? If you were quite low, that frightens you because something might have been missed in the process, but usually you get past all that and begin preparations for the production to begin. You put up a bond, which says that if your company does not complete this project, the bonding company will take everything you own. It's frightening, but it's something you grow accustomed to in this line of work. You must have quality people in your company and dependable machinery to make it all work. In our empire we were fortunate to have many fine workers and supervisors. It was a union town, and we pretty much had a handle on them because we were the biggest game in town. We had the asphalt plants, concrete plant, pipe crews, dump trucks, bridge crew, and all the earthmoving equipment necessary to build the biggest roads. All the best help flocked to our little empire in Illinois.

Things can and will go wrong on construction sites. One such project my dad was involved in was the shipyard debacle in Tampa. The shipyard was owned by George Steinbrenner, owner of the New York Yankees. Pete helped land that job, but George was forthright enough to warn Dad and Pete that they were quite low on their bid. Everything that could go wrong did. First, the company down south wasn't set up with the same quality help as up north to take on such a large project. There were more thieves on our payroll than there were in the county jail. They stole dirt, tools, steel, time, and any commodity that was up for grabs.

One day the crews painstakingly erected forms to pour a large wall for the dry dock. After pouring several hundred yards of concrete, the entire wall collapsed in a single second. Dad, standing by, could only watch as all the labor, effort, and money went down the drain for that day. Imagine how his ulcers felt that day! He became so preoccupied with that project one night on his way out to the beach house that he ran a red light at a major intersection and was nailed by another car. He easily could have been killed but was spared as the other car t-boned him at the rear passenger door.

The company lost $500,000 on the project. It's tough to recoup lost money; in fact, you never really do. You just have to lick your wounds and move on to the next project.

CHAPTER FOUR

Living with Success

Having a highly successful and visible family name was quite a perk growing up, but with any success comes jealousy. There was plenty of that among some of my classmates and even coaches at school. One of my football coaches, Len Tibby, would get on me during practice by calling me "moneybags." This was degrading, and I would have loved to take him out for a good whippin'. A good friend, Warren Provost, challenged the coach to a "duel after school," but Tibby turned him down for fear of getting his ass kicked.

As I was growing up, I began to see what political clout could really do. We had a good police department in Kankakee, but I should have been jailed several times in my mid-teens. One wintry night in January I was driving intoxicated and slid my car over some concrete bollards and almost totaled it. The cops came, assessed the situation, and put me into the custody of ... my father! I think getting a DUI would have been less punishment than having him deal with me. Hell hath no fury over an angry Sicilian. I was grounded about a month, and then I was back out partying with my buddies. Another incident came with a friend toting a beer in my car. I let him drive, and he peeled out going about sixty in a thirty mph zone. Of course the cops stopped us and found the beer. They made me go home, wake up my father, and call the police station. I must have driven Sam crazy with all my antics. I was in the dog house quite often in those days. Curiously, my driving record stayed clean.

My rebellion got me in plenty of trouble, but I was always able to wiggle out of it. I loved hanging around Greg, whom my father could not stand. This buddy of mine was a great source of inspiration to do evil things. We'd go shoplifting together, stealing pants, shirts, or belts at fine clothing stores. It was petty stuff, but how would that have looked in the local newspaper? A prominent area family with a thief for a son! Nanu would have choked me. Sometimes my buddy and I would get drunk and break into a house just to party. We didn't want to steal anything, just have a place to party. I once held a party in Raymond Hall, a non-descript storage building the company had cleaned up and named after Nanu. About seventy to one hundred drunken high school kids showed up—but no cops did. I was out of control, but there was no one there to stop me.

I often felt like I was on the road to oblivion. My grade point average was a mere 1.6 when I was a junior. I wanted to go to college, but how would I ever make it there with those grades? Of course, the reason I wanted to go to college was to party, but it took me two years to raise that GPA to 1.8.

Sports were a good outlet. During my freshmen year I played football, basketball, and baseball. I was a fair athlete, but I soon learned to hate the politics I was often up against. Our company often donated paving projects to our Catholic school, but I'm sure it created problems for me with many members of the coaching staff, and I often felt overlooked for playing time because of jealousy.

I thought I was a real stud in baseball, making the varsity as a freshman, but then I got demoted as a sophomore to the junior varsity. I was indignant but went and served my time for a while. Then, I made a deal with the coach, Irish O'Reilly, that if I consistently hit above .330 for two weeks he would bring me up to the varsity. I hit a couple of home runs and batted about .350, but he refused to bring me up. I was upset and felt the coach had reneged on his promise to me, so I quit the team, going against my dad's advice. I felt I had to do it to show my independence. Looking back, I realize it was probably a stupid thing to do, but at sixteen we all do stupid things.

I played one year of basketball as the starting guard on the freshman team, but at the end of the year I got passed over for the sophomore tournament team for an inferior substitute, so I refused to play anymore basketball. No coach was going to keep me down.

I did, however, love to play football and stayed with it for all four years of school. The sheer joy of trying to crush someone's skull really thrilled me. I read all the books by Jerry Kramer of the Green Bay Packers and learned to love to hate the opponent. I wasn't that big—only five feet, ten and a half inches, and about one hundred and fifty pounds soaking wet, but I made up for it in fury and anger. I think it's the only way to play the game. I never had any serious injuries in four years. Football is truly amazing. It's like the gladiators in ancient Rome, who fought to the death against one another. Football players have the license to unleash their innermost animal-like instincts. It becomes a matter of survival, crushing each other with violence that often causes serious damage to one's body and long-term ill effects. The average lifespan of a National Football League player is fifty-five, about twenty years short of the national average. In those days, I dreamed of being a pro football athlete, but somewhere around my last high school game reality set in and I'd had enough. That's when I discovered my love for golf.

Sam had bought me a set of golf clubs on my sixteenth birthday. I thought he was crazy because I had never thought of taking up that goofy game. I would often caddy for Dad but had no intention of ever trying the game myself. By this time, we had joined the Kankakee Country Club, moving up in the social circles in town. I took those golf clubs down to the course and got my first lesson, and it wasn't too long before I was hooked. It turned out that golf was my kind of game. It wasn't anything like the other sports I had played. There was no team to be a part of, no coaches, no practices, no politics, and no one pushing me but myself. I was good enough by my senior year to make the varsity golf team which was one of the better teams in the area.

Golf helped me find an outlet to my rebellion and passion I was looking for. I could excel, and I felt the sky was the limit. I wanted to be a pro someday, but one thing stood in my way—anger. My football aggression came out too often on the links, and in golf one cannot channel anger into a positive force. It destroys the player's game. It often did derail me, but I would always come back for more, always trying to improve. I thought Jack Nicklaus was cool, and I tried to emulate him in his swing and demeanor. I just didn't have his talent. By the time I was about twenty, I could break eighty on occasion.

I found golf to be a perfect combination of a social occasion and a cerebral challenge. The real challenge of the game is that it parallels life in so many ways. There is always that new golf course out there to be conquered, just as there are always plenty of obstacles in life to be conquered. The architect of the golf course challenges you to successfully navigate through the trees and over the traps and water hazards, and to judge the greens. It really is a stimulating sport, but so often people don't get it; they think it's boring or too hard or both. Many golfers have a low self-esteem about their golf game. They put themselves down about how awful their game is so they don't get too disappointed or look more foolish in front of their friends.

One of the real frights for most golfers is to play in front of a gallery. I think it frightens them more so than public speaking. It exposes how well they can handle their game while others are watching. Of course, most of the time no one cares to watch weekend golfers play, unless you have the cash and the guts to play in a pro-am event. I had the great fortune of playing with Arnold Palmer in a pro-am event in Tampa in 1988. The anticipation was overwhelming. I went into the men's locker room to feast on the cold cut lunch buffet, got a plateful, and went looking for a table. There was Arnold Palmer sitting alone at a table. I walked up and said, "You mind if I sit here?" He said, "No, sit down!" I sheepishly sat down, looked at him, and calmly proclaimed, "We're playing together," as if he really cared. But, being the kind man that he is, he said, "That's great," and I quietly munched down my hefty sandwich and chips.

When I was practicing at the driving range, I kept telling myself that this was going to be fun and I should just relax and enjoy it. When it was finally time to go to the first tee, I grew more nervous with each step toward the tee. Looking down the fairway and around the tee, I saw what had to be a thousand or so people in the gallery. It practically looked like the U.S. Open, and there was a local TV station sports reporter, Dave Wirth, wanting to interview someone about the prospects of playing with a legend. My partners declined, but I stepped up to the mic and took him on. He asked, "So, are you nervous playing with the king of golf?" I replied, "I'd rather just say I'm excited because it's a chance of a lifetime and I have to look at it as just another round of golf."

As I teed up my ball for the first tee shot, I just kept thinking, *Make contact with the ball!* And I did. I hit it rather well, but it went into one of the hazards. However, I made a nice recovery to make a bogey, and from then on everyone settled down and had an awesome day with Arnie. He's the gentleman everyone says he is, and that memory was the best ever on the course. I found it really fun playing in front of the galleries.

Our team didn't do so well that day, but that was of little concern. I got to play with Arnold Palmer, one of my true heroes. The next year, however, my brother Rick and my dad played with Chi Chi Rodriguez in the same tournament and won the whole thing!

Playing golf at the Country Club as a teen gave me a nice taste for the good life. I knew this was the type of life I aspired to—hanging out with the upper end of society. What I learned at a young age was that usually the higher up a person is on the social ladder, the nicer that person is. That would surprise many people because the wealthy are sometimes thought of as scrooges—money-craving con artists—but that is not the case. As I've learned in my own business, the higher you go, the nicer the people get. It's always better to talk to an owner of a company than someone at an entry level or a salesperson. I like to think that the person at the top got there because he is a genuinely nice person and it's much easier to get others to do things for you by being nice than being pushy.

I have played golf with doctors, the mayor, oil tycoons, car dealership owners, drug store owners, presidents of large corporations, furniture store owners, insurance executives, and many other higher-ups in the community. The friendly environment of the links and having beers at the nineteenth hole has helped me learn how to interact with these people.

In those summers out of high school, I'd play big shot on the weekends at the country club, but during the week I was just another laborer in the Azzarelli empire. I could only dream about being one of the big players in town. My main goal was to just fit in with the crew and not screw up anything. As a son of the boss, I found that difficult at times, even though everyone thought I had it made. The foremen would some-times resent my presence because they figured that I would discuss with the boss that night whatever happened during the day. If anything went wrong, they figured I would rat them out. It was uncomfortable at times, but I tried to have a sense of humor. We SOBs (sons of bosses) didn't garner a lot of respect. We usually were the butt of jokes. I remember one foreman making the statement, "They're gonna figure out which kid knows the least and let him run this thing." I could've come back with something cocky, but inside it hurt, and I just didn't know where to put that hurt. I took it to heart and I began to want to leave the company. Other people in the company showed more class and tried to help us the best they could, but being an SOB was truly a lonely experience.

I hated school, but going to college was going to be my ticket to independence—away from Dad, away from home, and away from Kankakee. It was the time of Woodstock, and I was desperate to get there, literally or figuratively. I wanted to escape. I was running from myself, my failures, and even from my family's success. I was trapped in my own idealism, looking for some great life, free from problems, one in which I could just be myself and not have to measure up to anyone's standards. I was a hippie at heart. I wanted something better. I wanted to be a success at something, but that was way out there in the future, a wing and a prayer.

CHAPTER FIVE
The Seventies

As the Beatles broke up and John Lennon was on his crazy, drug-infested ride with Yoko, the Azzarelli empire in Kankakee and Tampa was humming along with greater steam. Pete in Florida had hooked up with a guy named Edward Debartolo, the mall developer tycoon, and made the company millions doing the site work and paving in Central Florida. When we made our annual trip to the Gulf Coast, I could definitely see Tampa in my future, but how would I ever get there? It seemed almost far-fetched. I was so used to the mundane life of the Midwest, but I loved the beaches and the Sunshine State. I would make trips into Tampa to visit my cousins, who had better jobs than we had up north, and we would cruise the town looking at the southern version of the growing empire.

Tampa is about twenty-five miles east of the beaches and is well removed from St. Petersburg economically. Tampa is a working town and has grown primarily because so much industry has moved there to take advantage of a cheaper labor force. Florida is a right-to-work state, as opposed to a union-controlled area such as Chicago. The city has a rich history of Cuban and Italian influence, and a lot of that history can be seen in the buildings still standing in the neighborhood called Ybor City. Ybor was a cigar rolling capital in the early part of the twentieth century and drew many immigrants to the area searching for work. Many of the original cigar factory buildings are historically protected and reveal to a large extent how the town grew and prospered. At one time the cigar industry produced 100 million cigars per year. Later, machines replaced many hand rollers, but there still are several small hand rolling operations within the city. In the late seventies, a year or so after I'd moved to Tampa, I was commissioned by the Villazon Cigar factory to design and build a parking lot for the employees. It was exciting to deal with the manager, and he took me on a tour of the hand rollers and gave me a couple of boxes of stogies, which I gave out to the paving crew. We soon realized just how strong the cigars really were. I had a stoned paving crew that day!

Nanu came to Ybor City back in 1938 and eventually bought a house just south of the main drag, 7th Avenue. He would commute to and from Kankakee as the winter and summer seasons changed. Later, Sam would adopt the same lifestyle, as he couldn't stand the cold Illinois winters. But that wasn't until he was well into his sixties and he had bought a condo on the beach.

Jose Marti came to Tampa in the early 1800s and got the Cuban revolution going with his fiery speeches and pleadings to the cigar workers to donate 10 percent of their wages to the cause. It is reported that a secret message was rolled in a cigar and smuggled to Havana with orders for the revolt for independence to begin. There is a park commemorating Jose on 8th Avenue in Ybor City today. Fidel Castro also made an appearance in town in 1955 to promote his own revolt and received significant press coverage by WFLA TV and the *Tampa Tribune*.

However, the real thrust of growth came when Henry Plant connected Jacksonville with Tampa by railroad in the 1880s.

Then, shortly thereafter, he opened the Tampa Bay Hotel, which still stands just west of downtown and is part of the University of Tampa. In 1898 Teddy Roosevelt stormed into town, bringing with him about 30,000 troops. He made Tampa a big city virtually overnight. The troops were here in June, July, and August, when the heat is quite brutal. I could only imagine these troops staying in tents, getting eaten by mosquitoes. Only the officers could stay in the hotel, and even at that without air conditioning, of course. Tampa has been rated as the third-most humid place in North America and would never have grown anywhere near the thriving metropolis it has become without the invention of central air. The normal highs in the summer months are in the low nineties, but it always feels like it's at least one hundred or more, especially in July and August. Many of those troops returned to Tampa after the war and stayed to raise families.

In the late fall and winter the Tampa Bay area turns into a tourist haven, as the weather is lovely from late October through April. Tampa hosts the Gasparilla Invasion and parade, which is the town's version of Marde Gras in New Orleans—with the exception that it only lasts one day. That one day is reserved for all the elite and respectable people to stroll down Bayshore Boulevard drinking cocktails and dressed up as pirates, Rough Riders, or wenches of the Caribbean. In the seventies, the parade was quite small and always took place on Monday. Today, it is always on Saturday and the town really lets it all go, with more than 100 floats of all manner of variety. It has become a major bash for the whole region.

Tampa was a working-class town and the Azzarellis fit in there just fine. By the seventies the "good old boy" network was in place, and Pete had carved himself out a piece of the pie. Projects would be divided up, and we got our share within the rising metro area. Nanu couldn't have been more right on when he envisioned Tampa as a major growth area. The established Tampa "rat pack" really didn't want Pete around in the early days and tried to run him out of business. However, they didn't know how tough and crafty he was and that he would not be denied his place in the Tampa business scene.

Tampa has a small-town mentality framed in a large-city venue. It's easy to find out what's going on in other people's lives. I'm always running into an acquaintance at the grocery store, a mall, or a restaurant. And after living there for almost thirty years, I've come to understand that in the earlier part of the twentieth century, mobsters were close friends with those who had regular jobs or professions. They all grew up together, but some went off on another not-so-legal track. Not that everyone hung out with gangsters, but there was a fine line between the two sides of the game. Nanu was never proud of the fact that the Mafia was so closely tied to the Sicilian heritage. Whenever the word *Mafia* came up, he would put his index finger between his closed mouth as if to say he just didn't want to hear the name.

Tampa is a fairly progressive town in that it has an expressway authority always looking to build a road to get the residents around town more efficiently. It is constantly coming up with new plans to carve winding roads through neighborhoods that might help relieve congestion that comes with a boomtown. St. Petersburg and Pinellas County seem to be stuck in their own sprawl, with too many towns to communicate effectively and agree on anything. The traffic crawls at such a slow pace that if you're traveling through there, you'd better have a good stereo because you're going to be sitting a while. Pinellas County has twenty-two municipalities, and each one couldn't care less about the other or what their plans are. (However, all the growth has been great for employment and, of course, construction.) The main highway is U.S. 19, and I've seen bumper stickers that say "Pray for me, I drive U.S. 19." The highway now stretches from South St. Petersburg all through Pinellas, Pasco, and into Hernando counties, a stretch of about seventy miles. The traffic is heavy southbound into the urban sprawl areas in the morning, and the same effect occurs northbound at night. The planning in those areas was largely non-existent; developers pretty much built whatever and wherever they wanted at the time.

The downtown area of St. Pete has a quaint flair to it, and the waterfront is beautiful, with a pier jutting out into the water a couple hundred yards or so. The beaches are nice, and the city finally put a cap on the height of buildings to five floors to avoid the "Miami Beach" effect of one huge high-rise after another looming over the beaches. Pinellas County is the most densely populated county in the United States, with about one million people and almost no vacant land left to build on. It's surrounded by water on three sides. The city can't build in the water; the environmentalists won't let that happen.

Tampa has always wanted to be big-time. In 1976 the Bucs came to town, and with the arrival of the NFL, it was on its way. The Bucs were horrible, but we had a slice of the national spotlight that everyone in cigar city craved. Right across the street from the stadium stood a large mall, which had been paved by Pete and Bart, and we even had our own little compound in which to tailgate before and after games. Pete loved to party and would always bring the company motor home to the compound for the games. When the Bears played the Bucs, it became a big rivalry for the Azzarellis. Often, relatives from Illinois would come down for the game, and Pete would throw a huge bash after the game with massive quantities of food, beer, and booze consumed by family, friends, and business associates. Once in a while a Bucs player or coach might show up to join in the fun. Rock bands sometimes played at the bashes.

HIGH SCHOOL GRADUATION

Finally, it was my senior year, and my final football game came and went. I got my picture in the newspaper catching my final pass of my career that night. I always cherished that picture because I never was a big star in football, catching very few passes, but I really enjoyed playing the game. I was also proud that my dad had that picture on the wall in his office. Now, football was over and I had to move on to bigger and better things. In the spring of 1971 I finally graduated, and my dream of leaving home and being on my own was close to becoming a reality.

After graduation, I was fortunate enough to take a trip to Europe with a group of students from around the country. The trip was meant to be a combination of classroom study and historical sightseeing adventures. We flew to London and stayed there a few days, having a blast going to the pubs and sightseeing. Then we moved on to St. Andrew's in Scotland, the birthplace of golf and home of the original golf course where the game began. We had to attend classes in the mornings, played golf all afternoon on the historic links, then frequent- ed the pubs until closing, which, much to our surprise—and dismay—closed promptly at 10:00 PM. We spent two weeks doing this, then boarded a plane from Glasgow, Scotland, to Hamburg, Germany, the place where the Beatles honed their talents. Hamburg was a nightly haven for drunkenness and temptations from hookers on seemingly every corner. We never did check out the hookers, except for viewing, but the drunken part was a nightly routine. We were eighteen, and over there we were legal and took full advantage of it.

After a short stay there we went to Brussels, Belgium, where the nightly party continued. The bars served beer in steins that were like small barrels, holding about five pints in each one, so it didn't take many of those to keep us buzzed. We next visited the Scandinavian countries of Sweden, Denmark, and Norway. We had heard about topless girls there but never did see one. We did, however, have a great-looking blond tour guide on one of those gondola boats. Copenhagen, where Tivoli Gardens is located, was a highlight of the trip and a frequent spot to drink and socialize. Upon leaving those countries, we took a long bus trip to Paris. We all learned quickly that the French really don't care much for us Americans. Our tour bus pulled into a restaurant with a shop next door, where everyone wanted to go, but right in front of us the establishment quickly closed its doors. Everyone in France wasn't that inhospitable, but that certainly stuck out in my mind. The art and museums were nice, but I'd been out of America for at least five weeks. It was time to head back home.

On the trip I met a really nice girl, Patsy Woods, a down-home Texas woman who caught my fancy. She had that velvety smooth Texas drawl that I couldn't resist. I thought I was in love, and upon my return to the states, I began a twelve hundred-mile distance love affair by mail and phone calls that would last into my freshman year of college.

My poor grade point average in high school limited my options for college. Back during my freshman and sophomore years, I could not have cared less about school. I was afraid if I really tried hard and didn't succeed that I'd be a failure, and that would have been a real disgrace. So I covered it all up by not trying at all. That bad attitude caught up with me. While my friends were going to Eastern Illinois, Northern Illinois, or the University of Illinois, I applied to St. Ambrose College in Davenport, Iowa, where a friend of mine was going. But my application was rejected. That rejection hurt to the core. I applied to Loras College in Dubuque, Iowa, and got accepted. I was happy about that, but I really wanted to go to St. Ambrose. I told my dad about it, and he contacted a business associate over in Davenport who knew some people at the college. Weeks later I received a letter from the school saying that, upon further review, they would allow me into the school. Dad pulled some strings and got the deal done. I have always been grateful to him for doing that. That's how he was. He didn't make it easy for me, but if he knew I was really hurting or wanted something badly, he'd do anything in his power to help me.

That summer dragged as I worked for the family business in various capacities. I injured my knee playing volleyball at the Azzarelli family reunion, which put me in cast. My golf and work were over for that summer. As I would learn later, that injury would become one of the luckiest injuries I'd ever have. I spent much of that summer attending many White Sox games at Comiskey Park and just biding my time, waiting for the fall.

It may seem surprising that I didn't come to Tampa to go to school. Even with my grades, I could have gone to Hillsborough Community College. But I didn't want to go to Tampa—yet. I didn't want to be close to more family. I wanted total independence, and I got it—except that Dad was footing the bill. He always wanted one of his kids to go to college, and I was the first one to go full-time. My brothers, Rick and Ray, tried it but hated it and ended up in the service. Ray went to the National Guard and Rick went into the Air Force. So going off to college was a win-win—Dad was willing to pay the bills, and I was more than willing to go.

The only problem with college is that it's really more of the same. It's school! I had to sit in classes, listen to boring teachers, study, and pass tests. I decided, though, that there was no possible way I would flunk out of college and go back to Kankakee and work for the company. The thought of that motivated me enough to keep me above the Mendoza line for college—a 2.0 GPA. Actually, I was doing a little better than that (about a 2.6), and I was scaling new academic heights. I had one biology course I thought for sure I'd never pass, but I was thrilled to get my C and get out of there.

It was great living in a dorm for the first time, meeting all kinds of different kids from around the Midwest. College helped me realize that my little sphere of influence and friends was just that: little. I befriended guys who looked like Jerry Garcia, with super-long hair and beards, people I never dreamed of even talking to or associating with. This is where I began to develop my philosophy of life; it carried me on my journey through life to this day and hopefully beyond.

CHAPTER SIX
Growth

Growing up in the Midwest and with my Italian heritage, my attitudes were pretty closed-minded. My dad's family came out of the Great Depression era. They overcame assimilation into a new country and learning to speak a new language to achieve a higher standard of living than they could have dreamed. Their prevailing philosophy on life was to make money and bust out of poverty. They had to constantly prove themselves not only to their parents, but also to themselves and their peers. They had to show that they belonged here and could thrive here.

It had to be a large hill to climb, but for my dad it was a mountain that he continues to scale to this day. He wanted me to go to school to become better educated and because he only made it through eighth grade. The family needed his labor to help survive the Great Depression. After making it through that era, they surprised even themselves by how well they had done. By then, each one of the brothers and sister had large families. During their peak working years, as the men slaved away at the construction business, the women gave birth to thirty-four kids, the grandchildren of Nanu and Nana. Bart has since adopted one boy, Matt, which makes the total thirty-five grandchildren. That is quite a contribution to the baby boom generation.

Fate can deal us some devastating blows or delightful blessings, and ours were generally blessings—raising families in a small neighborhood, which created tight bonds among the cousins that have continued for the most part to the present. My cousins and I have all stayed fairly close and still enjoy seeing each other at our family reunion each July. In fact, we still control some property together in our land company, Azzarelli Development, a family company that was a vision of Nanu's as a benefit to our generation. It keeps us in touch with each other and makes us work together as a family, which Nanu would have approved. Over the years, we have sold off many pieces of land from the company and there really isn't all that much left to it—enough to keep a board of directors in place and the need to have a yearly stockholders meeting.

MASLOW'S HIERARCHY OF NEEDS

I feel strongly that our family in American culture was driven similar to Maslow's hierarchy of needs, which he introduced back in 1943. After bridging the gap from poverty and desperation, the next generation rises to assimilate into a burgeoning culture of an educated workforce. This new, rising culture looks beyond merely gaining a foothold in society to obtaining a new sense of autonomy and intellectual fulfillment. Most of the early 1900s immigrants and others were at the cusp of the Industrial Revolution, trying to establish themselves and emerge from the agricultural society that dated back to the origins of America.

The hierarchy of needs says that the basic needs of shelter, food, oxygen, and health must be met before anyone can move to the next level of need, such as that of basic safety— physical safety from violence and aggression. Nanu's family struggled at this early stage: at times they really didn't know where their next meal was coming from. Another need at this level is one of security of employment and that of revenues and resources. These two areas were significant in the stage in which my family was struggling during the earliest years in America. It speaks volumes to realize that it all started in two boxcars hooked together. That was *before* the Great Depression. At that point their basic need for shelter and food were barely being met. By the time the Great Depression rolled around, they were well-prepared to handle it.

In the next hierarchy of safety needs, my family had some security of employment, because they were such hard workers, but there was virtually no security of revenue and resources. That would come later with the establishment of the corporation and subsequent successes. The very biggest security they did have was that of family; they clung to each other and became the true basis of their success. In addition, they were all fairly healthy, and Kankakee was a small town in a rural setting with almost no crime to speak of.

The next hierarchy involves the need for love and belonging, which they filled at home and through meeting, courting, and eventually marrying their spouses. This is always one of the tougher areas to get a handle on. It's often understood that parents love their children, but the children don't always get the warm and fuzzy feeling that they are really loved because it is understood, not spoken. Once his love and belonging needs are met, a human being needs to be respected, have respect, and to respect others. The person needs to feel accepted and valued, especially in the business setting. This can be difficult if the person is still struggling with the bottom of the hierarchy emotionally. My family was really taken by surprise at the great strides they had made financially and socially. After many years of prosperity, the Great Depression was still inside of them, but they were much happier dealing with these strains than the previous strife they had experienced. This level of the hierarchy is more complex and tricky because of the various types of personalities involved in the process. As a person gains more notoriety, money, wealth, and fame, their true personality may or may not be able to handle the added exposure to the social and inner pressures from rising to such a high stature. How else can anyone explain Elvis Presley dying at forty-three from doing too many drugs? Or Jimi Hendrix, Janis Joplin, or Jim Morrison? The list goes on and on. Even a highly successful neighbor of mine committed a gruesome suicide by jumping off a parking garage at Tampa International Airport seven years ago. He left behind a wife and three boys. Many people need respect and reassurance from others, but often they have not accepted themselves first. No amount of money, fame, or fortune is going to make them feel good about themselves.

The next section of the pyramid is that of cognitive needs. After fulfilling his other needs, a person is looking to learn, explore, discover, and create in order to get a newer, higher understanding of the world around him. This is where I was in college, an idealist looking for a better way for us all to live together as one. I loved the peace movement in the late 1960s and early '70s; I never could understand why men wage wars and kill each other. There simply is no logical basis for that. I would always think, *Why can't everyone just get along?*

California Dreamin'

At Christmas break in late 1971, I had an opportunity to travel to California with a buddy and another guy stationed at Coronado, California. Dad was against my going, as I was only 18 and he could only imagine what went on out there. But I convinced him to let me go, and we shipped out in a van Bill Rosencrance bought in Illinois. He was a Navy diver who specialized in planting dynamite on bridge pilings. This guy was nuts, but we had a blast with him. We stopped in Fort Worth and got free lodging courtesy of the military. The next day we took off down Interstate 10 all through Texas, New Mexico, and Arizona. I had never been to all those beautiful places, and I thought I was in heaven.

One morning after sleeping in the rear of that van with no heat in the back, I woke to a mesmerizing sunrise across the purple-shaded Arizona desert. As we drove, we saw a hippy hitchhiking along the side of the road. He had a guitar, so Bill pulled over to pick him up. He was truly grateful and started strumming his guitar. He sang "My Sweet Lord" to us and continued to serenade us across the outrageously painted desert of Arizona. *Easy Rider* didn't have anything on us thrill seekers.

I'd never been to California, and I fell in love with all of it, especially the San Diego area and the weather in January. Back in the Midwest my family was in a deep freeze, while we hung out at the beaches with palm trees swaying from the breezes of the Pacific. Why would anyone want to go back to the frozen tundra? California was a true paradise on earth, a perfect combination of great weather, desert, mountains, and the Pacific Ocean always cooling the West Coast. It's no wonder the Beach Boys made millions writing songs about its ambiance. We made the trip up to L.A., where I had always wanted to go, but it left something to be desired for me. It was so large and spread out and smoggy as Chicago is. I was in love with San Diego. I started dreaming about making my way out there to chase my dreams after college.

We didn't make it to San Francisco, though I wanted to. That would have to wait until later on in my college career. In 1971, life was still a bunch of soft flowers and sunshine. The cry of peace was everywhere. Especially in California.

Chapter Seven

Vietnam and the Draft

The Vietnam War was exploding in 1971 and '72, and back in Davenport, Iowa, we staged a three-mile walk and sit-down protest in the middle of a downtown street. There were five hundred to eight hundred students who joined together and sang, "Give peace a chance." John Lennon and Joan Baez would have been proud—we were being true conscientious objectors. Everything was cool until some wise guy decided to throw a brick through a window of a downtown business. Then we were just kids afraid of getting arrested, and the whole crowd dispersed. It was easy to be idealistic because nothing was on the line for me. But it wasn't long before that changed.

The military held a lottery for the draft, throwing all of the 366 birthdays of the year into a gumball machine and picking numbers. Mine came up as fifty. I got sick over it. I didn't sleep for days, and all I could think about was going to the jungles and rice paddies of Vietnam. Now, my protest had new meaning. I could be going from being a naïve, idealistic student in the Midwest enjoying the exploration of the universe through my newfound freedom to packing an M-16 rifle with a bunch of other misplaced American kids in a frightful reality no one expected to confront at the prime of their life. Everyone said the first eighty lottery numbers would head to Southeast Asia. While all my friends talked about what new car they were going to get or what they were going to study the rest of their college days, all I could think about was my very uncertain future—or whether I even had a future.

It was a grim time in my life, but what could I do? There were plenty of others in the same boat. More than 58,000 U.S. servicemen were killed during the Vietnam War, and I began to wonder if I'd become just another statistic.

After getting the unfavorable report about the lottery, my interest in the war began to peak. I would watch news reports religiously to see if maybe this mess would end and I could go back to living a semi-normal existence. President Nixon seemed to want to get out of Vietnam as the country, especially us students, put the pressure on him. But he was caught in a squeeze, trying to gain victory and not abandon South Vietnam. He poured bombs on the north like crazy, hoping the Viet Cong would give up against our superior air power and negotiate a settlement.

As the spring term turned to summer, I went home and went through the usual motions of working on one of our construction crews, making some cash while I was carrying the weight of the ultimate question—what if? What if I have to go to 'Nam and cut short my dream of a destiny on the Florida coast? What if I don't find the girl of my dreams, get married, have four kids, and build my dream house? What if I don't make it up that Maslow pyramid toward self-actualization? I had so much I wanted to accomplish and felt so much desperation as I pondered these questions. I felt like a prisoner of the U.S. government. I was its property and it would call the shot for me. This was a living hell for me, as I greatly valued the independence that I was beginning to explore while away at school. Now, I was in a perpetual state of limbo and didn't know if a chance at real freedom would come again.

I would never support the war, but leaving the country as many did to avoid the draft was never an option for me. My dad and uncles served in World War II; their lives were interrupted, their dreams were put on hold, and they went to take care of business as directed by the military. It's part of living in our free society. In their war, there was a real threat to the world with the way the Japanese and Hitler were hitting us from both sides of the globe. Anyone could see after Pearl Harbor that we were caught in an undisputable wedge that we were going to have to fight through to keep our freedom. With Vietnam, however, it seemed that we were stuck in a jungle fighting a war with an unknown enemy, one that might be your friend by day and try to kill you at night. What could we possibly gain? The people of South Vietnam weren't even supporting what we were doing. Somehow, we believed we were stopping the spread of communism, the great, lurking evil we all had grown up fearing since the Joe McCarthy fifties. This seemed pretty irrelevant to me, and most of the country agreed. That summer Dad and I argued often about Vietnam. My father tended to agree with Nixon because he had always been taught that authority was never to be questioned. He believed that if everyone just did as they were told, it would all turn out for the best. I was part of the new generation, out to change the world our own way, and we had decided that war was not the way to do it. Down deep, though, I believe that Dad was as confused as anyone, because this war obviously had no real direction to go. We could not sustain our protection of the south indefinitely, especially since the support of the war in the United States was quickly fading.

As the summer dragged on and my mind was stuck on the war issue, I discovered a band called the Moody Blues. I bought a couple of their albums, and I was immediately engrossed in both the music and the lyrics that they imprinted upon my heart. They spoke of love, taking care of one another, experiencing a world where there was no greed or confusion about the value of your own self in the world. Some might think the band was way out there, but at that time I was way out there myself, looking for a world with some stability and the assurance that I would have a somewhat bright future. The Moody Blues provided a fantastic escape from my world of doubt and fear of what might come. One of their songs, "Voices in the Sky," really took me away: "Look what is happening to me, I lie awake with the sound of the sea, calling to me." The simple elegance of those words was very touching and delivered a mellowness I loved, especially when dreaming of my hoped-for future home.

When in Florida as a teen, I always loved listening to the waves at night with the windows open. The waves would lap upon the shore, one after another, lulling me into a trance— the constant, permanent, undeniable sea moving toward the shore, only to be stopped momentarily and sent back to where it came. I would easily fall into deep sleep. In those days, war and the gravity of the responsibilities of life were a few years off, which seemed an eternity. When I was a teen, each week seemed like a month, and a month like a year. Talking about a "year from now" seemed like an eternity away.

But in the summer of 1972, all I really had were those dreams, and the Moody Blues sent me to those places I wanted to be, where life could be special and we didn't have to hurry around pushing each other, trying to get ahead to the point where life was only about making money and having material things. To me, life was meant to be enjoyed, but I had little of that joy. I'd see the GIs on the nightly news and wonder if I was about to become one of them. My life was on hold, and I cursed that lottery daily. The winners in this lottery were the losers. Many of my close friends had high lottery numbers, such as 235, 320, or 187. It all just seemed so unfair! I felt like a loser, like there was something wrong with me, like a black cloud was following me around. Nobody that I knew had a number under one hundred. I felt that I was going through this alone, without a friend.

The annual Azzarelli reunion was to take place the first Sunday of August. The gathering is anything but a normal picnic. At noon we always have a Catholic mass. Back then, the mass was said by Father Tremonte, a local priest who seemed to me to be at least ninety years old, but was probably much younger. He would push the mass through in about twenty-seven minutes, record time by Catholic standards, as mass usually lasts at least forty-five minutes. After mass, everyone dives into the first huge helping of food. Our spreads could rival a cruise ship, except with a distinct Sicilian flair. Countless types of pasta, salads, and vegetables—so many that one plate is never large enough to hold it all. After scarfing that first wave of food down, we had games for the kids and beer and conversation for the adults. Back then, we would have pony rides for the kids, swimming in the pool, and the competitive egg toss, in which many would get splattered with the gooey yolk. The volleyball games at the reunions were quite fierce. The South would take on the North for bragging rights, and I, of course, was on the Union side at the time. This particular year we were having our usual battle, popping the ball back and forth, up and down, always looking for that weak link on the other side. I was playing the front line and, as usual, waiting for my chance to spike. What happened instead would change the course of my future.

I saw the ball coming toward me, and I jumped as high as my five feet, ten-and-a-half-inch frame would take me. I slammed the ball downward for a victorious spike, but on the way down I twisted my knee. As soon as I landed, I felt extreme pain, shockwaves going up my leg from my knee and a sense of buckling that I'd never experienced before. I lay on the pavement squirming and screaming, "My knee, my knee!" I couldn't walk without a limp and realized I had done some damage. I finished out the picnic, pigging out at least two more meals and guzzling plenty of beer to try to quell the pain that was exploding inside my left knee. It didn't dawn on me then that this injury was my ticket out of being drafted into the United States military.

I went to bed that night thinking that I'd just had a bad fall and my knee would be fine in the morning. But the next day my knee looked like a softball; it was swollen beyond recognition. I hated going to doctors, but on this one I had no choice. I went to see Dr. Morey Lange, one my dad's golfing buddies. He diagnosed my injury as a severe strain of the arterial ligaments that required an immediate cast.

My cast was full length, from the top of my thigh to my ankle, and the only way to move about was by crutches, something foreign to me. I would soon learn to adjust. I took a lot of pain pills, such as Darvon, which was the only one that killed the throbbing in my left knee. Work was out of the question, and I soon became bored hanging out at the house. Music was a great escape; the Moody Blues came in handy, along with James Taylor and, of course, the Beatles, my first real love of rock 'n' roll. I was able to go to some White Sox games, but it was a real pain trying to get around, and the August heat made it all the more uncomfortable. In about six weeks the cast came off, but the knee wasn't in that great of shape. It was still somewhat swollen and sore. Late in the summer I received my orders to report to downtown Chicago in November for my draft physical, which I had anticipated all along.

Returning to campus was bittersweet for me. The excitement of newfound freedom wasn't there anymore, and the constant reminder of the war pounded in my consciousness. Some reports seemed positive about a resolution, but I couldn't allow myself the luxury of not worrying about it for one day. I was the only one I knew going through this, and I realized then that the only real fact of life is that no matter how many people, places, or things we surround ourselves with, we are all relegated to aloneness in this world anyway. Without a faith based on trust in God, I really was alone in this world to face my ultimate fate. I wanted November to arrive and get it over with, but even the thought of the physical scared me.

In late October 1972, Secretary of State Henry Kissinger announced that "peace is at hand." That sounded great to me, but the army would still draft soldiers. I was hopeful that at least that I wouldn't go to Vietnam, but serving in the army or any service branch was not appealing to me. I always felt that if someone is personally called to the military, then go for it. It's not only noble but necessary because the United States will constantly have someone after us. The more good will we spread worldwide, the more we will be the target of plots to either take us over or destroy us.

In 1972 the troop levels were decreasing, but living through the first war ever caught on nightly newsreels, I couldn't believe the war would actually come to a conclusion. As I moved closer to my physical date, the negotiations Henry Kissinger headed had begun to unravel, as the Viet Cong soldiers from the north would not leave their positions in the south. One night I called my dad, explaining my pitiful position about my future. He said he had come up with an idea. He had talked to our family physician about my plight, and Dr. Schale said he would write a letter for me explaining to the military doctors how my knee was damaged quite badly playing volleyball and the prospects of it holding up under stressful combat conditions was doubtful. He would describe the injury in detail and maybe this would help me get released from my draft duty.

It was a gray, chilly day in November when I reported to downtown Kankakee and sat waiting for a bus to take me to Chicago. How many fun trips had I taken to the Loop, Comiskey Park, a rock concert to see Crosby, Stills & Nash, or even an auto show? It was surreal riding in a vehicle I never would have intended to be in. But there I rode, seemingly alone, but there were others on that bus. I was lost in myself, and my thoughts wandered about in pity and loneliness at the dilemma I was facing. The thought of the coming winter and its barren landscape depressed me even more so. Thoughts of the holidays gave me little consolation, considering the situation I was facing. At the same time, it was the springtime of my life. I tried to think of how the previous generation had fought WW II and how it must have felt that they were thrust into the middle of someone else's madness. So why should my burden be any lighter? Why should I get to have this cup taken from me? It was a good question, but still I wanted to fulfill my own dreams, not Nixon's.

The dingy green rattletrap bus eased its way through the middle-class southern suburbs of Chicago, past Comiskey Park, through the high-rise slum projects, and finally into the Loop. The usually beautiful city skyline seemed of no consequence on this day—just a dull, drab cityscape of my destination of duty. The bus pulled in the army headquarters and we were herded into the processing center. I had my letter from my doctor firmly in my possession, holding it as though it were that ace I could wait to play at the right moment to pull through a tight poker game. We went through all the usual physical drills—the urine specimen, the blood pressure, the testicle cough, and more. I gave my letter to a steely eyed officer, and I imagined what he might be like at my boot camp. He said he'd get the letter to the right person and that I would get my moment before the head M.D.

I was going through a series of tests and following the herd when a doctor told me to come with him. He took me into a separate room, away from my fellow potential draftees, and told me to lie down on the examination table on my stomach. He lifted my left leg upward, holding my foot and twisting it. I knew he was feeling for the stability in that knee. I felt it pop, and I know he did, too, so he did it again to make sure. In the latter part of the summer, after my cast came off, my knee would pop out of joint. At first I went to the doctor to see what I should do, and he showed me how to twist it back into place.

After that exam, I was returned to the herd. Finally, we came to a desk where everyone was getting their draft status. Those who were 1A would be assigned to boot camp. I got to the desk, and the sitting sergeant stamped on my manila envelope "4F." I excitedly and naively asked, "What does this mean?" He looked at me and deadpanned, "You failed your physical."

Never in my life had I been so elated to fail an exam, and believe me, I'd had my share. It felt like the jury acquitted me. A huge burden was lifted off my shoulders. They gave each of us a pass to go downstairs for chow, and I swear it was the best meal I'd ever eaten—roast beef and mashed potatoes. I was so excited, but I couldn't show it because so many guys around me were bemoaning their 1A draft status and the uncertainty that brought with it. Later, I boarded the bus with a completely new outlook on life. The sun came out, and I was thankful that my life was given back to me. Winter wasn't looking so bad after all, and I started thinking about all the things I wanted to accomplish in life. I was thrilled to get back to St. Ambrose College to get the rest of my life started.

Chapter Eight
On with Life

Soon after my failed physical, the election came. Of course, we college students put all our efforts behind George McGovern for president. It blew us away that Nixon kicked his butt. It was a landslide by modern standards. Nixon got 60 percent of the vote as opposed to McGovern's paltry 37 percent. We were extremely upset because we felt McGovern represented our new ideals for the future and Nixon was just the same old establishment guy with the same old worn-out ideas. It wasn't meant to be, and all of us liberal collegians were brought back to reality—it was still the "silent majority's" country.

The rest of 1972 sped by, and the war kept going. Nixon launched an all-out bombing campaign on Hanoi to try to get the Viet Cong to the table and end the war, but they wouldn't give up having their troops in the South. The bombing was halted only for Christmas day and continued until about the end of the year, but it was proving to be fruitless. In January 1973, Nixon sent Gen. Alexander Haig with a letter telling South Vietnamese President Thieu to put up or shut up. America would cut a deal with the enemy whether Thieu liked it or not, so he had better go along. They cut a deal, and on January 23 Nixon announced that a deal had been reached to end the war; there would be a cease fire in Vietnam, Laos, and Cambodia. We would pull our troops out and the North could keep theirs in the South. In return, the Viet Cong would release our POWs.

Soon thereafter, South Vietnam fell, which was regrettable but inevitable. The whole war was such a disaster. It had started with Kennedy sending a few advisors over there in the early 1960s and mushroomed into a major war that transformed a culture, creating a generation that began to constantly question authority rather than accepting it at face value. The Who wrote a song called "Won't Get Fooled Again," which said it all to me. When I was younger, it seemed like the older generation all knew what they were doing, but maybe not so much, as it turned out. But they still were in control; "Tricky Dick" was the man for four more years, so we might as well get used to it.

One thing Nixon did that I liked was to institute an all-volunteer army soon after the conclusion of the war. This helped him regain some popularity, but it was a little late. What about all those deceased soldiers, their families, and the guys coming back who were reviled rather than given heroes' welcomes? I had a friend from Kankakee who came back from the war and seemed fine, but he got cancer and died in his midtwenties. He told me about Agent Orange and how they used it to kill the foliage so the U.S. soldiers could see the enemy, but it was deadly. He predicted that many would die from exposure to it, and he was right. He was one of the casualties of the war, though he wasn't counted among the 58,000 who died in Vietnam.

After watching all that had transpired, I realized that what I had been through in 1972 paralleled what the country was going through. I wanted out of having to serve in 'Nam, and the country wanted out in the worst way. Nixon was feeling the heat. Likewise, the military, the rest of the country, and I were all melted in a convergence of dread at how this drama would play out. As the Doors sang, we all desired to "break on through" to the other side so we could move on with our lives in a somewhat normal fashion.

Back at St. Ambrose

After the war, everyone settled into the college routine as though nothing had happened. All of our anger and move toward activism waned, and it seemed that the wind had been taken out of our sails after the election and the end of the war. What was there to fight for now? Let's just get back to being sophomores in college and forget politics. Back at St. Ambrose we were more into listening to Led Zeppelin, Deep Purple, and Black Sabbath and flipping Frisbees around than taking on the establishment. Kent State and the war were now completely in our rearview mirrors. The discontented winter was turning to spring, and the sun would finally peek out in Davenport, an old river town on the Mississippi where the sun rarely comes out in the winter at all. I think it was less sunny there than in Kankakee, which I thought was impossible. I remember one stretch of at least two weeks in January where the sun was nowhere to be found.

That spring a lot of my senior friends were going to graduate. My roommate, Jim Smith, and I hung out with older guys because a good friend of ours from our hometown area was two years older than we were, so we got to know his friends quite well for those two years. Most of them were from Chicago and most of them loved the White Sox, not the Cubs. In Chicago, you love either one or the other, but not both. Cubs fans hate the White Sox and vice versa. Legend has it that the dividing line is Madison Ave., about in the middle of the city. Bugsy Moran ruled the north side and loved the Cubs. Al Capone ruled the south side and often went to old Comiskey Park for games. We all loved the Sox mainly because we were from the southern parts of Chicagoland.

Knowing our buddies were graduating, Smitty and I started

thinking about going to a different school the next year. It would be a huge step, but after staring down the prospects of going into the service and Vietnam, it really didn't scare me that much. I was up for anything. After our friends graduated, we went back to Kankakee and Manteno, Smitty's home town just north of Kankakee, ready to work for Azzarelli Construction for another summer.

Smitty and I went to the same high school. We were on the football team our freshmen year all the way through our senior season. We had a lot in common: similar size, marginal football talents, and marginal scholastic abilities (or willingness to put in the effort). We also fell for the same girl. Chris was the girl of my dreams during our freshman year, and I wanted to date her badly. But when I asked her out, she told me she dug someone else—Smitty. They dated all through high school and college. Today, they are still married, living in Washington, D.C. I had no chance, but it's just as well.

Smitty's dad died when he was young. I never met him, but by all accounts he had forged a nice business and personal relationship with my uncle John during his days up in the little town of Manteno, Illinois. He developed some land for which Azzarelli did the work. He also had a thriving insurance company. Smitty had two other brothers, and both of them at one time or another worked for Azzarelli on their summer breaks.

When I finally got accepted at St. Ambrose College, I knew Smitty was going there, and I felt it would be a nice way to ease into my first college year by rooming with someone I knew. On the enrollment form, it asked if I had any preference as to whom I wanted to room with. Of course, I wrote down Smitty's name. We ended up together in East Hall, and he always figured it was by coincidence and still today doesn't know about my little scheme. We weren't close friends in high school, probably because of my secret admiration for Chris, but in college we became inseparable buds, hanging out and doing everything together like brothers. Some of our college friends thought we were twins. Smitty was quite the lady's man back then, but through college Chris stayed true to him, always writing him, holding onto her dream of being with him forever. I was jealous that he had a girlfriend who was away at another school and still so in love with him. It was my dream, but I remained without a steady girlfriend through college. The timing just never seemed quite right and I was fine about it.

While we were at St. Ambrose, Smitty's brother Denny was at Notre Dame, where his oldest brother, Francis, had graduated previously. The family ties to Notre Dame were extremely tight and continue today. They are football season ticket holders and benefactors as well. We made one trip to South Bend for a game, and I soon realized this was not just another football game; it was total football passion at its highest level. Watching a game at Notre Dame is like trying to describe the ocean—you just can't, but when you experience it, you'll never forget it. On the Friday night before the game, we went to the bars, then to the huge bonfire and pep rally, where there were two thousand revelers. Up on stage as the emcee for the rally was none other than Denny, Jim's brother. He incited the crowd to a great frenzy, a fever pitch of football euphoria and leading perfectly to the moment when he introduced everybody's hero and superstar, Coach Ara Parseghian. The coach commanded unbounded respect from the Irish followers, becoming one of the true icons in Notre Dame history, with Knute Rockne and Johnny Lujack. Ara had won the national championship in 1966, and he would do the same in 1973. It was a moment to cherish, especially being so close to the players in the drama.

Later that season, Denny, Jimmy, Francis, a couple other friends, and I flew to Miami to go to the Orange Bowl. Notre Dame played Nebraska. It was a crazy New Year's weekend with these guys, as we partied down in the warm climes of Florida. Irish fever had taken hold on me as well. The team came out flat and got trounced 41-8, but I was hooked on Notre Dame football. Denny made it into Notre Dame by sheer will and determination. His high school grades fell short at first, so he went to Marquette University in Milwaukee. He earned the required grade point average and then transferred to Notre Dame. All the Smiths achieved great financial and community success, and Denny was right there with them. His charming sense of humor always made me feel comfortable, and we became close friends. We worked together in the summers at Azzarelli and spent many nights on the town in Kankakee and other venues. Recently, Denny passed away after suffering from a long battle with ALS, and it hurt me to the core to lose him.

EARNING RESPECT ON THE JOB

The summer of '73 was a year of transition for both Smitty and me. We had lived in the Midwest all our lives, studied at St. Ambrose for two years, earned 2.5 GPAs, and felt ready to discover new vistas. Many of our best friends had graduated college and were moving on. I looked at going to a new school, possibly the University of Arizona, where my new girlfriend, Linda Koch (from Kankakee), was located. In August, I traveled to Tucson to see her and check out the school. It was an awesome place, with the mountains, palm trees, and desert. It was also hotter than anything I'd ever experienced in my life. Every day the thermometer was reaching 105 to 110 degrees. It was so hot that I needed a handkerchief just to touch the car door after it had been sitting in the sun for a while. Arizona was fantastic, and I began considering it as my future home. But, as fate played out, things didn't work out between Linda and me, so I headed back to Illinois to finish out the summer pondering my options.

Back home at the annual family reunion, I saw one of my favorite cousins, Nora Azzarelli, and we started talking about Colorado State University, where she was attending. She described how great it was living at the foothills of the Rockies with the great climate and wonderful hiking, skiing, and the grandeur of the mountains. She said the school was awesome, with friendly people cruising around on ten-speed bikes. CSU had about sixteen thousand students—not too big, but not too small—whereas St. Ambrose had only twelve hundred students, many of them locals who didn't live on campus. I craved the increased social life that a university would bring. Besides having football and basketball teams, it was much more of a cosmopolitan campus.

I became excited about the prospect of Colorado State even though I'd never been there. I wasn't a big fan of cold weather, but the mountains still sounded like a great place to live for a couple of years. After the reunion I gave Smitty a call, and we talked it over extensively. Both of us decided to send our transcripts to CSU and fill out an application for admission. Surprisingly, we were both accepted within two weeks, so we got together, had a few beers, and decided to go for it. Of course, we first had to discuss it with our parents, as we had never entertained the idea of going to school such a great distance from home. Smitty and I were Colorado-bound, at least in our minds.

That summer I worked full-time on a crew building the west wing of St. Mary's Hospital in Kankakee. It was one of few times I'd worked with the building division of our company, and I grew to like it quite well. My labor foreman was a tough, no-nonsense guy named Jerry Palmateer. He reminded me of a drill sergeant—broad shoulders with a stiff upper lip—but fortunately, he had a great sense of humor. He'd walk around all day singing, giving guys grief if they didn't perform—or even if they did. He treated everyone the same. He had thought that I would act like most SOBs (sons of bosses)—spoiled, showing up late, knowing we couldn't get fired, and generally acting like a pain in the ass. I vowed to prove him wrong. I did show up late a few times, however, much to his disliking. I heard about it from him in no uncertain terms, so I decided I would start showing up on time and work my butt off. I wanted to earn his respect if it killed me. In fact, I actually did get hurt three times that summer, although not severely. One time I lost control of a wheelbarrow and fell on top of it, jamming the handle into my chest, which created a huge lump on my breast. Another time I had a wheelbarrow above me as I was spreading stone in a ditch. A backhoe loader backed into the wheelbarrow, crashing it down on top of me, stone and all. A third incident happened when I carried too much plywood across a small plank bridge and I lost my balance and fell into the ditch head first. I think those accidents probably happened because I was trying too hard to prove myself worthy as a worker to Jerry.

By 1973, I was twenty and my physique was filling out. I felt like I was starting to come into my own as a person. Jerry treated me like a human being, and I was gaining his respect. That was important to me because he was a real company man. It was the first time I felt the need to prove my worth, since being an Azzarelli in the company owned by my dad made others think we were given an easy road to travel when it was just the opposite. Everyone else got respect, but not the Azzarelli boys. I could see the genuine company spirit Jerry exuded and I wanted him to approve of my efforts. By the end of the summer he told me how I had really surprised him with my excellent work ethic, and he wished me well at college. We had become good friends, and I had gained a measure of self-respect that I had never had in the workplace.

CHAPTER NINE
Out to Colorado

In September 1973, Smitty and I were on our way to Colorado. I drove my blue Oldsmobile Cutlass and Smitty had his maroon Ford van. We had spent so many hours partying in that carpet-covered van the last couple of years that I felt attached to it myself. On the way out we made a short stop at Davenport to see some old friends and party there one more time. It was fun, but we were both eager to move westward and expand our horizons. We headed out on I-80 through the rolling hills of Iowa, the flatlands of Nebraska and, surprisingly to me, the extremely flat terrain of eastern Colorado. Once we entered Colorado, we thought, *Finally, we're here!* But the drive from the state line to Fort Collins, home of Colorado State, is more than a hundred miles with very little to see in the way of human population or even service stations. Pity the poor fool whose car breaks down out there! And that was before cell phones. Finally, after at least fifteen hours on the road, we began to see the massive Rockies in the distance. We both started honking our horns and waving our arms out the window. We were rejoicing that we had arrived at our next station in life, one that held so much promise for a new day and a great escape from the nasty Midwest winters. We had no idea where we were going to live, but it didn't matter—we were in Colorado, a place I could have only dreamed of calling my home a few years earlier in high school. I truly felt free, even though I knew there was school to attend and plenty of work to be done.

We went apartment hunting immediately and ended up in an ordinary apartment complex on the west side of town, but it was close to the mountains and the view was great. We looked for roommates because we rented a large, three-bedroom apartment and we wanted help paying the rent. We saw an ad on a cork board at school from two girls looking for a place, so we called them. After much discussion about how awkward this could be, we decided to give it a try. Imagine that: Smitty, me, and two chicks in an apartment together. It sounded too good to be true to all of our friends, who imagined there'd be orgies on a nightly basis. It was anything but that. Sue had a steady boyfriend and Anita seemed pretty cold in her demeanor. Still, the four of us developed a friendly, platonic relationship for the school year.

Smitty and I started meeting a few friends here and there and got to know our next-door neighbors, Steve Van Hook, Guenther, and Corky. Corky had a steady girl, so we rarely ever saw him, but Guenther, Steve, Smitty, and I became good friends that first year. We spent countless hours listening to the Pink Floyd monster hit album "Dark Side of the Moon," which played out as the soundtrack of our lives. Steve was nicknamed "Tex" because he came from the small oil town of Canadian, Texas, where his dad worked in the oil industry. He would play a big part of my life from then until today.

Adjusting to a larger school and living on the outskirts of town was somewhat of a challenge. St. Ambrose was so small that the classes were all within easy walking distance, and it was easy meeting people. Once we got settled into our new surroundings at Ramblewood, our apartment complex, we began to meet some of our neighbors in the complex and hit it off pretty well. I've always liked to have a few close friends.

I tend to form lasting bonds and develop a real loyalty to my friends, keeping in close contact over the years.

In those first months in Colorado, Smitty and I took many trips to the nearby mountains and sampled the night life every weekend in Fort Collins. We had one friend, Mark Guimond from Kankakee, who dropped in one night and ended up sleeping on our couch for about five months. We called him "Heavy" for obvious reasons. He liked to call himself "ramblin' man" because he drove sixty-five miles to and from Denver every day to work in the shoe department at K-Mart.

For the most part the first year at CSU was good and the weather was better than back in the Midwest. In the winter, the days were usually in the forties and sunny with an occasional frost or some snow, but nothing like what we Midwesterners thought it would be like in Colorado. Most of my friends and family would ask about how much snow we got, and they would be surprised to hear that it rarely did snow on the foothills. It wasn't uncommon for me to be out playing golf at the local municipal course in the middle of February. The grass was brown, but I never had the chance to play golf that time of year in Iowa or Illinois. Of course, many winter mornings we'd look to the west to see the gleaming Longs Peak covered with a fresh glaze of snow. It was truly a beautiful sight, and we never got tired of the mountains and their majesty.

The mild winters was a nice surprise for me coming from the dreary Midwest, and fall in the Rockies was a delightful time of year too. Up in the mountains, the aspen trees turned yellow and the cooler breezes blew in, making it great for hiking, which I was soon doing frequently. It seemed no matter where I wandered off to, I found a new, exciting vista to explore. I was seeing God's handiwork and beautiful creation, and it was far beyond what I had expected. As a kid, I'd always known there were places like this, and I knew

someday I would reach these destinations—and now it was
all coming true.

Turning 21

In the spring of 1974 my twenty-first birthday was coming,
and I started to get the idea that maybe I'd drop out of school
for a quarter. CSU operated on the quarter system rather
than semesters. My dad and mom flew out to see me for
my upcoming birthday, and I went down to Denver to pick
them up at the airport. It was one of the times when we got a
big snowfall. It started snowing as I drove down, and it kept
snowing until about twenty-three inches fell in the span of
two days. We never made it back to Fort Collins. My parents
were on their way to Las Vegas for the Florida Road Builders Convention and had to fly out. Odd, isn't it? Florida road
builders would go to Las Vegas for their convention. I guess
they liked to gamble and party.

While visiting with my parents, I told my dad about my desire to take off a quarter, and he didn't like the idea at all. But
after much convincing, he seemed to understand. When it
came time for them to catch the plane to Vegas, he turned
to me and said, "You want to go?" Are you kidding me? He
was asking a college kid if he wanted to go to Vegas. I didn't
even have a change of clothes, but we were on the next plane
south. I did, however, have my golf clubs (the most important
thing). We bought some clothes in Vegas, and we spent about
four days partying and gambling dad's money away. I soon
found out just how much stimulation is constantly thrown
at visitors in that city. I played poker at Circus Circus, losing
my shirt while watching all the animals in their cages and the
trapeze artists doing their thing. It was weird, to say the least.
Then Dad and I played golf at the Las Vegas Country Club,
and that was the highlight of the trip. Not a bad twenty-first
birthday present.

I headed back to Fort Collins to try to find a job. I easily found my first job away from Azzarelli at a small concrete company, Kiefer Concrete. After starting the job and working harder than I ever had at my dad's company, I wondered what the heck I had done. I had gone to school, did a minimum amount of studying, and got by with a 2.6 GPA. What was I thinking? Why take a semester off to work a hard job? It was too late by then to get back in school. I'd been out of school for about ten weeks when I realized that I'd better go back as soon as I can.

Hiking and Golf

Being young and adventurous can get a person into trouble, especially when hiking. My friends and I would travel to places in Colorado where the hiking was beautiful but also treacherous. One such spot was Rawah Wilderness, a special, little-known area hidden in the backwoods. Mike Larsen, Smitty, and I went up there for a little hiking on a beautiful Saturday morning. The peaks were quite impressive, and Mike took off by himself on his way to the top. He was a Colorado boy, and he had far more experience than Smitty or I. We didn't really know where to start or how to climb these large peaks. After about an hour we looked up to the top and saw Mike there, yelling to us and telling us how great it was up there. Smitty didn't care to take on the challenge—he was much too sensible for that—so I headed off alone. I climbed about one-third of the way up the mountain where I encountered a large boulder field. There were some huge but loose rocks, and I soon found myself in increasingly precarious positions. Every step seemed like a dangerous and frightening move. If I made one wrong step, I could lose my footing and fall a hundred feet down, tumbling to a certain death. It was pretty scary and I prayed, "If I can just get out of this mess, Lord, I'll never try this again." I decided then and there that peak climbing was not for me. I eventually made my way back to the guys with a few cuts and bruises, not to mention a bruised ego, and had to hear it from Larsen about how it easy it was and how could I not make it to the top, but I didn't mind. I was just glad I made it down.

Other trips to the mountains were more my style. One of them included visiting Estes Park, a tourist town at the gate of the Rocky Mountain National Park. There is a nice golf course there where the golf ball would travel about twenty yards farther than at sea level due to the more than mile-high altitude. I played with a couple I didn't know because none of my buddies at the time played golf. Everyone was busy doing their own thing, but my first true outdoor passion was and still is golf. This guy was hitting every fairway, every green, and at the end of nine holes, he had shot a par thirty-six. I shot a pedestrian forty-two, and I knew it was going to be tough to overcome this golfer.

After getting some refreshments, we went over to the tenth tee. His wife went up next to the women's tee so she'd be ready to hit her tee shot. My competitor (in my mind) teed it up, looked down the fairway, stepped up to the ball, drew back the club, and smacked it … hitting a low, hard duck hook shot that hit his wife in the upper right back and making a sickening, thud sound in that large muscle above the kidney. She screamed and moaned, writhing in pain. It was one of those moments when I had to ask myself, "Did that just happen?" He wanted so bad to help her; luckily, the ball hit in a spot where there is plenty of muscle to cushion the blow, and she could try to walk off the pain. At first I thought they'd go to the hospital, but she insisted she'd be all right. He wanted to quit playing, but she insisted they keep going. She had a large welt in her back, but she knew her husband was playing the game of his life.

Not anymore. Understandingly, the husband now couldn't hit anything straight. Nothing went his way at all that back nine. He shot a forty-seven, eleven shots higher than the front, and I shot forty on the back nine, beating him by one shot. It was a hollow victory for me, seeing his wife bravely trudge through the last nine holes and him being shook up over what had happened. Golf is an emotional game, and those who play must have the "feel" of the shots to be successful. On the front nine, that man was truly "in the zone," where everything is comfortable and producing the desired results comes naturally. After such an upsetting moment, there is no way to achieve that "zone" again. Losing the zone can easily happen to any marginally talented amateur and even a professional golfer. We've all seen accomplished players have a meltdown on the last hole of a big championship, losing the tournament because of nerves or mental distractions. Getting ahead of yourself in golf can be disastrous. Each shot has to be played one at a time, no matter how cliché that may seem. I hold pro golfers in high esteem because of the mental strain they must endure, although it looks like such a simple game to the casual viewer.

Colorado Quirks

Back in the foothills, Smitty and I were gaining a new found love for bluegrass music. I had always been a pure rock fan—the Who, Rolling Stones, Led Zeppelin, and the Beatles were my favorites—but we attended a couple of bluegrass festivals and it really got in our blood. Everybody there loves to drink beer and get up and dance like fools. It was really fun and quite a change of pace from our rock 'n' roll roots.

One of the great quirks we found was in a tiny town called Severance, east of Fort Collins. It was a fitting name, considering the only bar-restaurant in town was Bill's Restaurant and Tavern, where the main feast was that of beer and Rocky Mountain oysters. If you're thinking that has anything to do with seafood, you're wrong. They are the testicles of a castrated bull. Bill made a great living for about fifty years at that bar, and it gradually became a tourist stop as well as a local favorite.

At the end of our first year in Colorado, Smitty and I were

happy with the friends we'd made and our GPAs. In early June we decided it was time for a road trip, as seen in the movie *Animal House.* This road trip, however, was a lot longer. We loaded up in Smitty's van and, just before heading out, pleaded with Steve Van Hook to come along, but he told us that the money just wasn't there so he couldn't make the trip. We planned to head out I-80 west to San Francisco, one of my dream destinations. We cruised out through the mountains, crossing the Great Divide, which always intrigued me: all of the water flowing from the divide going east goes to the Atlantic Ocean, and everything flowing west goes to the Pacific Ocean.

We made a short stop in Salt Lake City to see Guenther's girlfriend, Etta, then got back on the pavement for the long ride across the salt flats, into Nevada. Lake Tahoe was like heaven itself. Finally, we entered California, passing through Sacramento and Modesto (where the wine is fine) before arriving in the splendid San Francisco. Nothing I'd seen was quite as beautiful as the city itself, with the rolling hills created by the earthquakes. The higher we went up, the better the fantastic views were, especially of the Golden Gate Bridge and surrounding area. We finally made it to Haight-Ashbury, the center of the love movement about six years earlier. We were, as Jimmy Buffet sang, "arriving too late." It had become a tourist destination, a place where visitors went to remember a bygone era. We wanted to experience all the other special destinations the Bay area had to offer. Point Reyes National Seashore was a strange and surreal spot about thirty miles north of the city. It shows the real California—how it was hundreds or even thousands of years ago—as it remains an unspoiled spot along the Pacific Coast Highway. It reminded me of Pebble Beach, which I'd never been to but had seen on TV while watching the Bing Crosby National Pro-Am. If Smitty had played golf at the time, we would have had to make that trip to play golf along the ocean.

After several days of playing and partying in San Francisco, the funds were running a little low, as it is quite expensive out there. I looked at a credit card my dad had given me, and it showed on the back it could be used at the Best Western Hotels, so I figured we'd give it a try. It worked. We stayed in a big, round hotel right in the middle of the city. It extended our stay a few more days, so we took in as much as possible, including the Golden Gate Park, Muir Woods, and Sausalito, a quaint little village just north of town over the Golden Gate Bridge. I had my chance to eat buffalo meat, which was quite tough, but tasty and not as jaw-grinding as Rocky Mountain oysters.

I didn't want to hear too much grief about the credit card balance, so we headed back to Fort Collins and eventually home to Kankakee. I felt satisfied that I had now seen all three major metropolitan areas of California and a nice chunk of the west. I was building a nice travel portfolio of choice destinations for my life's album to someday talk about with my kids or even grandkids.

CHAPTER TEN

Returning to CSU

Returning to Colorado State University in the fall of 1974 proved to be quite interesting. We had more friends, felt more comfortable in our surroundings, and found a six-bedroom house at 714 Remington Ave., just east of campus. Six of us lived there: Steve Van Hook ("Tex"), Smitty, John Guenther, Hutch, Heavy, and me. Hutch was a total trip unto himself. I don't think we ever really knew his first name; he was just "Hutch." He was the opposite from the rest of us. He was trying to become a geotechnical engineer. He never partied, always studied, and was very serious about his future. We kidded him to no end, but it was good to see someone have an idea of what he wanted to do after college. One night we persuaded him to party with us, but he just couldn't hold his liquor. He was hammered after about three drinks and passed out before the party got going. I think he was hung over for about two days.

We held mega parties at the house and eventually became known as the "gang busters," a term coined by Tex. Tex, Smitty, and I played on a flag football team with a former Notre Dame quarterback, Pat Steenberg. We won every game except the last one, the state championship. But we had good times with the guys and partied after the games.

That entire year guys would come and go; new roommates replaced old ones as friends started to graduate and move on with their lives. Our house was like a revolving door of roommates, which was neat because we met a lot of people like this. We went to all the football games. The CSU team stunk, but nobody cared—we just tailgated, and by the end of the game no knew or worried about who had won or lost. One snowy game, students started throwing snow balls at the referees. One got hit in the head and started bleeding, and the announcer threatened that they would stop the game and make us forfeit if we didn't stop.

My cousin Nora lived a mile or so down the street and would come by for parties and football games. Little did I know that my roommate Tex was smitten with her, but he never could get close enough to connect with her. That winter, Smitty's oldest brother, Francis, and a couple of friends came out west, and we all took a wild trip up to Vail, the hottest skiing destination in the state. I wanted to ski, but I remembered the doctor warning me about my knee disintegrating below me if I made a wrong move. (I guess conservatism was starting to set in.) I never did try skiing. I stayed close to the ski lodge's hot pools and bars with Tex, who didn't ski either. He was too uncoordinated, I think, but since he had spent much of his young adult life in Colorado, I thought he'd at least try.

That spring before we graduated, Smitty and I finally coaxed Tex to go with us on our final spring break. This time we jumped in my blue-and-white Oldsmobile Cutlass and cruised south on I-25 through Denver, past Pikes Peak, through New Mexico, into Arizona—stopping at Winslow, made famous by the Eagles in "Take It Easy" (our anthem)—down past Tucson, and finally crossing the border to the Gulf of California and the little poor town of Nogales, Mexico. I'd never seen Federales before. These police meant business. They rode around in World War II vintage jeeps with semi-automatic machine guns looking for punks to give them trouble. I made a wild turn in front of them, and they gave me a look that made my heart pump faster. Thankfully, we found our hotel just in time. It was a crude little village, but the beaches were soft and mellow with the soft waves of the deep blue waters gently lapping up in the vibrant Mexican sunshine. At night the town was pure chaos, with wild Mexican bands playing and students dancing until dawn and drinking tequila. We made it safely back to the states and I chalked up another nice trip to my travel portfolio.

That May we all bid farewell to Smitty, who was ready to graduate. He went back to Kankakee, where he worked for my dad's construction company. We'd stuck together four years and never once had a cross word with one another.

That summer I stayed in Fort Collins, enjoyed a nice summer at the house with some new acquaintances, and that August took the strangest trip of all. It was between the summer and fall quarters, and I had a couple of weeks to hang out, so I went down to Aspen to do some hiking. Pulling into town, I felt like Clint Eastwood, hanging my hat at an old-fashioned hotel with hardwood floors, a brass bed, and a porcelain bathtub. Immediately, I packed my gear and went hiking toward the mountains called the Maroon Bells—three massive peaks set behind three crystal-clear lakes on a day so perfectly sunny a postcard couldn't do it justice.

I trudged onward as if to find the secret to life. I felt like it had to be right there behind those peaks. I was on a mission to go all the way around them and back to Aspen, a walk of at least twenty-six miles. I had walked at least seven miles when I reached the point where I could go up a peak or turn around. It was as if the mountain was issuing me a challenge: can you handle it? I had to try. I started up the trail. It wasn't as dangerous as the boulder field I'd faced before, but as I went up, the sky turned dark. As I got to the top, it started to snow—in

August, no less. After ascending the peak, I started down the other side, and it stopped snowing and began raining. I was wet, cold, and hungry. At the bottom of the other side, the sun came out and it was nice but cool. I had just experienced all four seasons in the matter of about two hours.

Hiking further on, I saw a cloud with lightning coming *up* at me. This was a little frightening because there was no place to hide. I was completely exposed to whatever was going to happen. The lightning passed right by me, and I soon spotted a tent below me. It was as if I was on a desert island and saw a search plane. I was saved, spending the night with a guy and a couple of girls. The next day I went back the way I came. My adventure was over, and it was my last major hike in the Rockies.

GRADUATING AND GOING BACK TO WORK

Going back to Fort Collins, I felt ready to make my way through my final quarter of school. Life beyond the ease of school and creative loafing was calling me. I wanted to go on to my true purpose. It was the fall of 1975. I was twenty-three and ready to take on the world. After an uneventful fall, I got my Bachelor of Arts degree in Social Sciences, and I was within seven credits of getting a degree in psychology as well.

I said good-bye to whoever was living at the house at the time and steered my Cutlass east on I-80 with my head full of sentimental thoughts about my college years—the knowledge and experience I'd gained and the friends I'd met. I cherished everyone and realized how lucky I'd been to not go into the service. I thought about how many people would never see all the sights I'd seen. I drove across the barren plains of Nebraska, Iowa, and Illinois. It was December, not my favorite time of year. Some depression was setting into my soul that winter. The stark reality of the workaday world was upon me, staring me in the face. It was the holidays, but my mood was strangely dark that year.

Everything that was certain was now completely uncertain. What was I doing in Illinois? California was awesome, with the ocean so blue. Arizona had the purple mountains in the sunrise. Colorado's sky was eternally blue, with the stark contrast of the pines in the hills. But I was back at my starting point, my hometown, as Bruce Springsteen sang. I was hurled backward four and a half years, feeling somewhat lost and overwhelmed. I went back to work at the family business. Dad had promised great things to come—someday I would be part owner of the company with my cousins. I wasn't sure it was the place I wanted to be.

I worked a couple of months, sometimes in temperatures as low as ten degrees, which seemed absurd to me. The local union had a rule that if the temperature dropped below ten degrees, no one went to work, but if it was right at ten degrees it was okay. Sometimes zero and sunny felt good if there was no wind, but rules being what they were, they couldn't work. Another day might have gusty winds and a wind chill factor of negative twenty, but if it was ten degrees, we had to work. Sometimes it felt like Siberia.

Going back to work for Azzarelli was an ambivalent time in my life. I had no real conviction about achieving anything there, so there was nothing pulling me to do my absolute best. Part of me wanted to accomplish great things, but I needed something to give me hope. I was just going through the motions, as many college graduates do, not yet willing to put their best foot forward, still holding onto the easy life of college. I felt I could be doing better than laboring on a concrete crew.

Hawaii

My brother Rick and I packed our bags for Hawaii in mid-February. The winter already had been too long for me. We planned a two-week excursion, and the days dragged on waiting for departure day to come. We boarded a 747 at Chicago's O'Hare airport with palm trees swaying in our brains. As we boarded the plane, however, we noticed the plane was full of retirees. It was a chartered plane—no wonder the price was so cheap. There were only two younger people on that flight, but they were both girls. The plane winged out of the frozen tundra of Chicago, stopped off in San Francisco and then jetted out over the Pacific for the four-hour flight to paradise.

As we arrived in Honolulu, the scenery immediately captivated me. This was better than any place I'd been to. The mountains were close by, the water was crystal clear, the beaches were powder soft, and the weather was warm and breezy. We went to our hotel, the Waikiki Hilton, right on the beach. The next day, there was a tour bus headed for the Punch Bowl, where thousands of soldiers from World War II were buried with other prominent Hawaiians. We got on the bus with about fifty other people, all of whom were sixty-five and over. Rick and I looked at each other—no way were we going to stay on that bus. We got off and went to a rental car establishment, loaded up our golf clubs, and headed out on the coastal highway. The views were stunning traveling around Diamond Head as we headed north along the coast and found a golf course. After a round of golf, we loaded up the car with beer and headed up to the north shore, which is famous for the fantastic surfing—not for us, mind you. We just sat up on the hills and watched the surfers do their thing. It was interesting to watch blond-haired beach boys risking their necks for the thrill of the ride. I had tried surfing on the small waves of Waikiki Beach earlier in the vacation, and since I couldn't even get close to standing up, I had to admire their skills.

The next day things were a little more interesting. We went to a public golf course in Honolulu to get eighteen in before cruising. We noticed that every person at the course was Japanese, including the head pro. That didn't seem like a big deal until we stood at the counter waiting for help. The pro at the counter completely ignored us, even after we pleaded to him to take our greens fees. I had never been discriminated against before. My dad told me about being called a Wop, Guinea, or Dago in his younger days. It really pissed me off, especially knowing that about thirty-four years earlier, the Japanese had bombed Pearl Harbor, and now it seemed they were running the town. There is some prejudice in everyone. I think it's just part of being human, but when it's acted upon, the results are hurtful and damaging. We loaded up our clubs and headed west to Pearl Harbor. There we checked out the Arizona memorial, then headed over to the Pearl Harbor Country Club, where we were welcomed and played on a nice course with beautiful views of the ocean and surrounding mountains.

Hawaii is made up of more than 130 islands, and few people know about most of them. The main islands of Oahu, Maui, Kawai, and the Big Island are about all most people know of the chain. We didn't really care about all those other islands either, but we knew we were ready to get off this one. The next day, we flew over to Maui and things got more interesting there. We stayed in a little cabin right on the Pacific Ocean, which was quite romantic—but not with my brother. After one night just hanging out and drinking beer, we finally hooked up with the two girls we saw on the plane. We had some laughs talking about the strange situation we were all in with the retired tourists. Our walks on the beaches in the moonlight were romantic. We spent countless hours during the days playing golf courses and fun nights partying with the girls. It was everything you'd expect a Hawaiian vacation to be, especially for two twenty-somethings on the prowl.

One night as we hung out on the beach my brother Rick

panicked. He wanted to leave Hawaii and go to San Francisco to see some old friends he knew from his military days at Travis Air Force Base outside the city. He wanted to pack up right then and fly back to California, spending a fortune in the process, just to have some good times. He almost had me convinced, but reason set in and I talked him out of it.

The next day we headed to the Big Island of Hawaii. There are almost no beaches, as the whole island really is just a large volcano. We stayed in the town of Kona and played golf on a course surrounding the big hole with steam coming out of it. I didn't want to be on the fifth when the darned thing erupted! The final day was depressing. Rick wanted to get back to see his girlfriend, Vicky, in Kankakee, and we were stuck in the little town of Hilo. That place looked like something out of the movie *MASH. They should film war movies here*, I thought. It was pouring down rain, so we just sat in a bar and listened to "Feelings." It was rank. We were both ready to get back to the mainland, even though that meant going back to Kankakee. So we jumped back on that 747 and flew back over the big blue. Back to our Siberia.

Chapter Eleven

Back with the Company

My real future was about to begin. I was going to be twenty-three years old in April, and I felt like it was time to make something happen. It was both exciting and terrifying, even though I knew I could always have a job. Many people thought that I had an ideal situation, but I believed the opposite. The company was a ball and chain to me. No matter what I did, it would never be good enough. The next generation was coming on board, and our fathers didn't have a clue how to assimilate us into the company. Sometimes I think they didn't really want us in the company and were threatened by our emergence from childhood to adulthood. The feeling of not being able to ever do enough to prove my worth to them frustrated me, because I held each one them in such high esteem.

Joe was my hero when it came to business. His tenacity in the boardroom always impressed me because he didn't take crap from anyone. He led by instinct, and his Sicilian hard-headedness made him seem invincible. Even Nanu saw his vision and leadership as vital to the future of the company. Nanu put him in charge and told the others to listen to Joe, which in some ways made things hard for him, since some of the others secretly and sometimes openly held grudges against him.

I always admired Johnnie's bravado and arrogance in dealing with the older brothers. Even though he was the younger brother, he felt that he had to "show his ass" at times to make sure they didn't shove him around. That's because he didn't know much about the construction business until he was in his thirties. He was my direct boss once I made the choice to go into the roadwork division of the company in the spring of '76. There was no uncle-nephew relationship with him; it was strictly all business with Johnnie. He was the boss and he intimidated me. He was about forty-six and knew enough about the business now to impress me.

I was always afraid of Bart. He seemed a little crazy, as if there was always a volcano rumbling inside of him. He had no love relationship with any of his nephews, and maybe even his own sons. He was a chain-smoking workaholic who had a large part in the success of the Florida division of the company. I admired Bart's ability to get things done and make money. But if I had wanted to try to please him, I just had to look at his own son, Bart Jr., to realize even he couldn't do enough to please his father.

I always admired Pete's ease in dealing with customers, his ability to get in front of people who would do him the most good. I also admired his ego. He was arrogant in the boardroom, letting no one get the best of him. He gave loads of crap back to Joe when he felt threatened. I liked the fact that he was willing to move to Florida and blaze his own trail—that enthralled me—and I wanted to have that quality in myself. He and I had a somewhat congenial relationship in the small amount of contact we had over the years. One time I heard him say he thought I had a lot of common sense. Compliments such as these were unheard of in our business family. No uncle would ever let on that he thought any of the nephews had any thing positive going for them. I think they thought that would be implying in some way that their own sons might be less than that nephew and that might hinder his future in the company. Ultimately, this thinking was the undoing of the Azzarelli Construction Company.

Of course, of all the brothers, I knew my dad, Sam, the best. There was plenty boiling inside him, but he didn't have the bravado to stand up to Joe and the other brothers. I think he felt underappreciated by his brothers, but he still busted his ass to make money for the company. Dad worked the drag line cranes, digging ditches often after working hours to make headway on the job. He was a true construction man in every sense of the word and was never afraid to get his hands dirty and work with the common people. I like to think that I have that quality, and I give my dad the credit for it. I realize that the guys working in the field are really paying the bills with their sweat, so they deserve my respect and to be treated well. Dad always pulled for the underdog, the lonely guy, the poor fellow nobody cared about—he always had a soft spot in his heart for these people. Once, when one of my sister's friends was going down the wrong path in high school, Dad agreed to pay her tuition at a Catholic school because he knew her parents couldn't afford it. He would do those things from his heart, not for recognition. But there was another side to him. When he came home he would take his anger and frustrations out on my mother and the rest of us kids. Things don't always go well on the jobs, and he often would bring those frustrations home with him. We all had to learn to live with his temper.

These players were the leaders of the company that I was coming into and thought I wanted to be a part of. However, it always felt like I was on the outside looking in, like the Moody Blue's sang in "Legend of a Mind." Early in the spring of '76 I went to work on an interstate crew, jack hammering out bridge approaches. It doesn't sound glamorous and it wasn't but, I got my white hard hat. This was symbolic to me in that it showed that I was in charge; a crew was now under me, not the other way around. It was only a three-man crew, but with it came a responsibility, paper work, and communication. I relished the opportunity. It seemed like a giant step forward for me, and maybe I was starting to rectify some of my screwups of the past. I also had the idea that maybe my life could take a more creative turn.

Music and Me

At eleven years old, just about the time the British invasion was a happening, I decided to take drum lessons. My older brother Rick was in a band, and I knew I wanted to do something musical. The drums enthralled me as I watched Ringo Starr pound out those skins. I was never the outgoing type—I knew I couldn't be the front man—so the drums seemed like a natural spot for my personality. I went to the lessons and found out just how boring it could be to learn the basic one-two-three-four beat on a rubber pad used to teach the basics of drumming. I went to about seven or eight lessons and quit going out of sheer tedium. However, the next Christmas I received my first drum set. It was a non-descript pearl-colored set, but it was a real set of drums. Before that, I had made my own set consisting of a snare, which I had used in practice sessions after the rubber pad, two toy tom-toms, and a round saw blade for a cymbal. It was a joke, but I would play every night to records that were popular at the time. We had a huge speaker downstairs, and the turntable was upstairs, so I'd put a stack of 45s or a couple of LPs on, run downstairs, and pound on my "drums," trying to pick up the beats. After getting the real set, I was ready to play some serious stuff. I would play during countless winter afternoons, beating away my winter blues. I was starting to get fairly decent at the basic rock beat, and I had a vision at that time of becoming a big time rock 'n' roll drummer.

A couple of years later Dad bought me a set of Ludwig drums, the same brand Ringo had, and I thought I was in heaven. I put together two different bands, and we had very limited success. One time I got to play with Rick's band, which was quite successful, winning the "battle of the bands" twice, which consisted of about seven or eight groups taking turns to duel it out onstage. His band, the Dark Shadows, had a fairly nice following locally, playing at weddings, bars, and high school dances. It was only one night; their regular drummer had to be home for curfew because he was on the basketball team and had a game the next night. The thrill of playing on stage was electric and made me want to make this a regular gig. It also gave me that little bit of confidence I needed to know that I could do this—there was virtually no stage fright for me.

My own bands never did become successful, though I did play in a group with Mitch Kiefer and Tom Gleason, brothers of the lead singer and drummer of the Dark Shadows, but we just weren't that good. Back in grammar school I played with a trio of Little League friends in a band that did play one gig at a roller skating rink, and that was about all. So I left my drums at home when I went to college. However, along the way, I asked for and was granted permission by many a night club-wedding band drummer to sit in for a song or two. Showing off my drumming skills in front of my friends always was a hit, and it boosted my ego a bit. When college took me to Colorado, I hauled my drums out there to fill in time between classes and once got a job in a disco dance hall, where they hired drummers to keep beat to the music. After one night, however, the manager realized I was straight rock drummer with no jazz experience and wasn't ready for the complex beats of John Bonham in Led Zeppelin. He let me go, so I took my $15 and went back to the house to keep practicing.

The drums are the sexiest, most sensual part of the band. The beat makes the room move if people are dancing and keeps the music tight in a rock band. Many of the great rock songs start with the basic beat of the base drum, snare, and high hat. "Start Me Up," by the Stones, is one example; Charlie

Watts pounds out the beat, getting the group into rhythm, and breaks the ice right off the top of the song. "When the Levee Breaks," on Led Zeppelin's fourth album, has another awesome drum intro.

So much of my formative years were bonded by music, with rhythm and blues roots transformed by my heroes into rock 'n' roll. In college, listening to music virtually became life itself, especially on cold winter days when friends would gather to pass around a few joints, listen to tunes, and let the day slip away into its own universe. The pot would bring the music alive: Jimi Hendrix was a whole other experience, and the Moody Blues were mind-bending under the influence. They made me realize that I could probably join a band, head out west, and get lost in the San Francisco or L.A. scene. That would be the ideal life—doing as I please, getting high, playing music, and living on my terms.

It wasn't long after I began working for the company full-time that all these thoughts started to come to the forefront. Was I copping out on my true calling, being a drummer in a band? Should I pack up my Ludwigs and head up to Chicago, get an apartment, and try to blaze a path to rock stardom? These questions haunted me daily. I knew there would be tough times and disappointments along the way, but it was no cakewalk in the family business either. I knew my music skills needed honing, but so do everyone's at one point or another. I had the Beatle's music down. The Who's, Rolling Stones', and some of Hendrix's stuff was easy. I could handle Crosby, Stills, and Nash. I knew I would improve with the right guys. It would just take one break to go my way, and there I'd go, off to the big stage, lit up and juiced up with adrenalin and ... other stuff.

That's the part that frightened me. I loved to get juiced up, and I had done my fair share of smoking dope. Drugs such as LSD, speed, mescaline, and MDA were always around back in the early 1970s, but I never fully embraced that scene because

I had heard about the mind-bending effects of these chemicals and I was afraid of their long-term effects. Pot was the norm for me and my buddies at school. It was always a spiritual experience, one that heightened my senses and made the music seem more than something to dance to, drink to, or just socialize with others while listening to it. I liked the feeling of being a part of that music. But I also realized in my pot-smoking days that I had become quite lazy due to its effects. Often I didn't want to go to class or just really didn't care about much of anything but listening to music, which hampered my grades.

However, after college the smoking days were pretty much behind me. It was 1975 and I recognized one clear fact: Jimi Hendrix, Janis Joplin, and Jim Morrison were dead. Three of my favorites died from either drugs or alcohol or both. This stark reality made me realize that drugs and music could be a deadly combination. The substances and the music had become one with each other. Partying continued beyond the concert, and the participant never could recognize when it started or when it should end. The years 1965–1977, in my opinion, saw the creation of the best music of all time. It was created in a state of heightened euphoria, where the senses were peaked and the imagination had come to life.

Music was my safe haven; I could always count on it to give me a warm and fuzzy feeling. It helped me know there was life beyond the darkness that pervaded my soul. I knew these brief interludes couldn't be physically good for me, but I was young and felt okay about it at the time. I always felt, even in the most intense pot-induced moments, that I would move past this time and not continue on a destructive path. Maybe I was lucky; maybe just naïve; maybe my guardian angel was really there; or maybe my mother was saying rosaries for me just as Nana had done for Sam in World War II.

I was in my own war, one within my mind, trying to find the difference between the idyllic me and the real me, the person God wanted me to be. The idyllic me just wanted to have fun, but at what expense? Going too far with all this stuff? Trying to live like there was no tomorrow? Taking everything to the limit? Trying to experience everything at another psychological level? Looking at life with blinders on? Thinking everyone should live, as John Lennon said, with "all the people sharing all the world"? It sounds so good, why can't we just share all the world? But Lennon, as I read in his interviews with *Rolling Stone* magazine, took LSD more than a thousand times and tried heroin as well. He built a multi-million-dollar career before experimenting with all these chemicals, and to some extent he did fry his brain. He was murdered in 1980. Where did the fame and fortune get him? Searching for fame has ruined many lives—everyone adores the seeker but he often hates himself. He wants the adoration of the people and the wealth that goes with it, but when he gets it, he often finds an empty world with no privacy. George Harrison was quoted in the book *The Beatles* that he never bargained for the famous life. He hooked up with arguably the two most talented songwriters in the history of music. George probably never would have made it big without John and Paul, and that might have been fine with him. He went on to a more spiritual existence and did charity work for others, so he saw that there was more to life than sex, drugs, and rock 'n' roll.

Another hero of mine was the great Jim Morrison, who died at twenty-seven. Some may think he was crazy, but was he really? He was searching for that alternate reality that railed against all traditional existence. I wanted to live life on my terms and make my own rules, yet I still valued a traditional existence (wife and kids). When I was a kid, the sky was blue and it never rained in my little sandbox of life. Music had a way of taking me to that little sandbox of safety, where no one judged me and I was king of my domain.

All of us have that war going on, but everyone deals with it differently. Morrison's song "Break on Through" talks about just that—getting to the other side. But what's the other side? Is it death? Is it the destruction of your mind, your being, your faith in God, or is there another possible breakthrough?

I had to come to terms with exactly how I would break through. Would I go on to be a superstar drummer, or would I fall back into the workaday world everyone else seemed to settle for after their college years? It was time to make my call. We always feel when we're young that we've got all kinds of time and there's no hurry. But as Pink Floyd said in the album, "Dark Side of the Moon," "And then one day you find ten years have passed you by."

Everyone wants a job with some sense of security. Once they get the job, often a wife and kids arrive. Maybe this is part of their dream. Once the decision to follow this ordinary path has been made, then the "window" has closed. Playing music and making it big is unique because the window of opportunity to do that is small. Being young without a family that depends upon you affords you the opportunity to give it your best shot at stardom. If a mistake is made in regard to the core purpose of your life, it may be rectified, but not easily. Going back requires more introspection and adjustments—reversals that take more valuable time off the clock of life. As I was making my decisions, there was absolutely no way of knowing the outcomes; but as I recognized the windows of opportunity, I walked through them in some kind of blind faith, knowing somehow I'd make it work. Or perhaps there was someone else walking through life with me. As I look back, I think it was the former.

Once anyone moves onto the chosen path, this question must be addressed: Am I happy doing what I am doing? It's not just a rhetorical question; it's the difference between being satisfied—or not—getting up each day, going out in the world, working with the seconds, minutes, and hours you've been given so you can develop a philosophy of life for positive action and an attitude that affects future generations and those who carry on your legacy. Will you gripe about why you didn't start that business or follow that music gig, instead settling for a rut that seemed "safe" at the time? Facing all these issues was both intriguing and frightening to me.

Entering into the music world was very enticing because I believed in my talent and I felt I would be true to myself. But something inside me told me not to go there. The stories of musical legends always seemed to have one common thread—depression. I already had a tendency toward it; maybe it was genetically passed down to me. The booze, drugs, and craziness of the rock 'n' roll life might easily have led me down that road, quite possibly to destruction.

CHAPTER TWELVE
Seeking Answers

Upon much soul-searching, I came to one important realization—I needed some help. Going to a psychiatrist or psychologist felt somewhat extreme, but I had a lot of questions and was searching for answers. So after looking in the yellow pages, I found someone to turn to. I did not want a referral because I wanted no one to know what I was up to. In my family, getting this kind of help was taboo or a sign of weakness especially since, as one of the more elite families in town, we weren't supposed to have these problems. But studying quite a bit of psychology in college, I knew there were people who could put an objective slant on my turmoil and give me some much-needed insight to the dilemma I was facing.

I picked a psychologist in a faceless office building on the north side of town to go to find the ultimate reason for my being here and what I needed to focus on—in other words, "What the heck should I do now?" We talked for our obligatory hour about how I wasn't sure about working for the family or if I should go be a rock drummer and how confusing it all was to me. It was somewhat surprising to hear myself say that I wasn't sure about working for my dad's company. I had been told since high school that we, the next generation, were being groomed to take over the company. I was in the middle of a thriving enterprise; why would I want to leave and not be a part of the excitement, the growth, and the money? That question haunted my soul. The last word is usually money; that's why I had to stay. It would be easier to thrive and enjoy life in the manner I had been accustomed to. Dad had given me all the material possessions and experiences I could have dreamed of up to that point, and I was only twenty-three. How many other twenty-somethings had seen all I had seen, done all I had done, or looked to such a promising future? I almost felt amused that I would even consider something other than working for the family.

But there I sat in a give-and-take session with a total stranger, searching for something, anything, that would give me some inkling as to what it I wanted out of my life or what I was willing to put into my life to capture depth, meaning, and fulfillment. I completely masked my deepest fears about my role in the company—feelings of anxiety, depression, and in-securities and how utterly overwhelmed I was about working with my father and uncles. I couldn't go to those dark places in my mind at that time, so I never let on to the psychologist, or anyone else, about my true feelings. This was going to be my only visit, I had no plans to be psychoanalyzed or anything as frightening as that.

Then the psychologist said one sentence that jarred me: "Well, you could start your own company."

At first that seemed far-fetched both to him and me, because even in the confines of his private office, I was a minor celebrity since my last name was synonymous with construction in the area. We were the standard for any and all civil engineering projects undertaken in our area of Illinois. Something moved within me, however, when I heard those words, something very frightening, exciting, and rebellious, even though I knew it probably would never happen. How could

I start a company, however small it may be, and stare down my own family in the same line of work? What would they think, and what would be the odds of survival? They would all hate me, I supposed, thinking how arrogant and ridiculous it would be when they had "paved the way" for me and my generation. The idea didn't seem remotely achievable.

My one hour was up, and I knew I dare not make another appointment. I knew I didn't want to get to the root of my true self after all, so I paid my fifty bucks and left. I guess going to a psychologist made me feel less than "macho," even though I'd taken thirty-three hours of psychology in college.

I was firmly entrenched in the esteem needs part of Maslow's hierarchy. I had so much respect toward my uncles that it generated a feeling of being overwhelmed when it came to the family business. On the other hand, my need for respect was unmet as each father in the family, worried over losing ultimate control of the company for his own son, could not show any respect for his nephews. No matter what any one of the younger Azzarellis accomplished, it would never be enough because all the factions in the family were fighting for control in their own way. Maslow writes that at this level, in the absence of esteem, people become susceptible to loneliness, social anxiety, and depression. I was trying to climb up a corporate ladder with no rungs. With all the apparent advantages in the world, I felt quite alone, much like a rudderless ship floating at sea with no pertinent destination in sight.

Still, as I walked out of the psychologist's office, I decided I would stay with the family business. It was just more convenient than pursuing the rock thing. As much as I loved the rebellion, danger, and thrill of the challenge of a career in rock music, I heard a voice calling me to settle down and see what would develop in regard to the family.

So I worked with crews and took in the small pleasures that came my way in the small burgh of Kankakee.

LOOKING FOR A MATE

My next goal was searching for the right mate, a woman who would love me for who I was, not what she thought I had or might possess in the future. In some small way, my search was like a movie star looking for someone who sees past his fame and public persona to find love for its own sake. I was no movie star, to be sure, but my family was very well known in our little town. I never took women too seriously in high school or college. There were flings here and there, but mostly those were about the thrill of the chase. I asked one girl who I dated in high school, Mitzi Bergeron, to get serious. She agreed, and the next day I called her to break up with her. That seems pretty bad to me now, but there was no way at that time I was going to miss out on any good times with my drinking buddies. It's almost like I had scripted everything back in childhood. I envisioned this really fine lady, blond or redhead, to be my wife. We'd have four kids and live happily ever after. As Cat Stevens sang, "I'm lookin' for a hardheaded woman, someone to make me do my best." But in high school and college, it was way too early for me to commit to a relationship. In those days I felt I had to be the wild man—rebellious, out on the fringe, going after all manner of hedonism while knowing that "real life" still lie ahead. There would be plenty of time to face all of those challenges.

One of my first experiences with love came with a woman named Linda Koch when I was twenty. We partied seriously that summer when I was home from school, and I had one of my first sensual moments with someone I thought I loved. I chased her out to Tucson to be with her in the late summer, but I first told Dad that I wanted to marry her. He did his best to hold his laughter inside because he knew she was not marrying material for me, but I was going to give it a shot. We had a blast together, but our affair would end soon. Our breakup was hurtful for me. She was blond, blue-eyed, and someone I had designs on being with forever. Getting over that first love is like pulling part of your guts out and laying them on the table for all to see and laugh at. I felt played for a fool. One night I was with her in a bar when she saw an old friend and started to make out with him! I wasn't man enough to walk out on her; I just sat there feeling totally degraded. Yet, I drove her home that night and kept dating her!

My first experience at what I thought was love explained my willingness to put up with being treated like dirt. Linda almost could do no wrong in my eyes, even while my friends were telling me she was crazy and asking me why I was with her. Hindsight is always twenty-twenty, but when you're young and in the middle of something as intense as that, mistakes can happen. It's easy to see how anyone can marry the wrong person. When you're in romantic love, you're out of control; you're irrational. You think she's better-looking than she is … in fact, she's perfect! And when this love is withdrawn, it is devastating. There is nowhere to put the hurt. When Linda pulled away from me, I was devastated. But somehow I moved on with my life.

At least I had this experience to draw from as I searched for my soul mate. I wondered how I would ever find the right girl in the small city in which I had been raised. It seemed impossible. Surely, most of the desirable girls had been taken, and even if there were one, would I be too shy to start a relationship? The dating scene in the 1970s repulsed me as it seemed so superficial. However, I would have to press on even in the face of my shyness and fear of rejection. I started asking anyone out for a date who seemed the least bit interesting. I was on a mission and could not be stopped.

The Dale Carnegie Course

In the late winter and early spring of 1975, I started taking the Dale Carnegie Course for public speaking. Dad recognized the shyness factor in himself, me, and my sister Mary, and he insisted that we go through this training. I was petrified at the thought of having to give two talks in front of at least twenty-five people once a week for fourteen weeks. Little did I know that it would set my course for a lifetime.

The course is a lot more than giving speeches and gaining confidence. It teaches a philosophy on life that Dale Carnegie lived by, one of treating others as you would want to be treated. The Golden Rule may sounds like a cliché, but attempting to live by it is no easy task. In fact, it's the kind of thing that alters your destiny, which I'm sure is how Christ intended. When you treat people the right way, it sets up agreeable circumstances for both parties. You wind up helping others to get what they desire, and that is far more valuable than it seems. When you help others, you help yourself as well. I had seen enough of the wrong approach within our family business—beating down others to get results—and I had internalized this enough to know that it produced some very negative results: anger, frustration, resentment, and anxiety.

Each week of the course taught a different concept of how to treat others correctly. *How to Win Friends and Influence People* was not only the motto for the course, but it was also the name of the handbook we studied during the fourteen weeks. Each student had to speak about their experience with the topic that was discussed the previous week. We had to apply what we learned from the instructor and the book as we went along. For instance, we had to praise another person's effort at work without appearing to be phony. That was difficult for me because we were always taught in the family business to "chew someone out" for doing something wrong. At first when I tried this new concept, the recipient of my praise would just look at me as though I was crazy. Even so, I noticed that it seemed to work to a degree. Another lesson taught us to be enthusiastic, and we had to act that way. I had always looked at work as drudgery, but then I remembered working with Jerry Palmeteer back in '73 and how I admired the vitality he put into his work. I started applying this approach to working with my crew, and we seemed to pick up the pace because of it.

Much of the course centered around the ability to lead others. I had never thought of myself as much of a leader; but considering my situation within the context of the company and the community, I started to think that developing my leadership skills would be a valuable asset. Once, my seventh grade teacher told my dad that she thought I had the makings of a leader. Maybe so, but back then, I was usually trying to lead others astray. Another valuable aspect of the course was learning to inspire others. If I were to lead others, I would have to learn how to inspire them about my vision and get them as excited as I was about moving in that direction. We also had to discuss building relationships, which is vital, not only in business but in families as well. I was determined I would have a family someday, and I wanted that relationship to be as solid as the larger family I had been associated with since birth. As Nanu always said, strong family unity is important. I knew I had to attain this; it was my destiny.

Each night the instructor would recognize the best talk of the night with a prize, and I soon realized that the winners were the ones who gave the most emotional speeches. For example, some students talked about dealing with the death of a parent or the illness of a sibling. This helped me to understand that my emotions were powerful tools with which to cope with life. Expressing myself with deep emotion was far more effective than scratching the surface with small talk and acting as if I didn't care. Even though this kind of expression made me feel more vulnerable, because risking anything means there is a possibility of failure, it is worth the effort. I began to realize that all these years I hadn't really put forth my best effort because I had been afraid to fail. People think that the ultimate defeat is trying really hard and not making it, so they wind up trying half as hard so that they don't feel so bad if they fail.

For example, I once wrote a paper in college about the SLA, the radical group that kidnapped Patty Hearst in the early 1970s. The student who wrote the best paper had to give a talk about the subject. I came to a point in the project where I saw a brilliant way to put a unique slant on the story, so I derailed the idea on purpose out of fear of giving the talk. I got a B on the paper. The Dale Carnegie course showed me there was a better way to approach life, and that is from the positive point of view. Whatever you might undertake, you have to think that it *will* work. You have to stop listening to all the naysayers around you who remind you about the pitfalls surrounding your efforts. Get past it and drive forward to the goal!

One critical session in the course included learning and remembering names. I have failed often at this important people skill, but it is critical at the right time. If you want to get someone's attention, there's nothing like speaking that person's name. Using the person's name shows that you are interested in him as a person. The key to remembering the name is to see that person doing something that correlates with his name. If a person's name is "Doug," you try to imagine that person with a shovel digging up the ground. It sounds crazy but it works; your mind sees the action and the name sticks.

Taking the course gave me a sense of confidence I never felt before. I had taken one speech course in college and had to give only one talk. When it came time to do it, I imitated Richard Nixon. People always got a kick out of me impersonating him, and it gave me a mask to hide behind without having to face an audience. But at Dale Carnegie, I had to face all these people as myself. After a few times up there on my feet, it strangely became fun to speak in front of others.

All in all, the course not only taught me a great deal, but it helped shape the person I became.

CHAPTER THIRTEEN

Falling for Mary

As spring approached, my search for the right woman pressed on. I had several dates with various girls that led to nothing, but I was never disheartened, even though I knew the prospects in that small town weren't plentiful. One Sunday in March I went to a sod party, a get-together where friends help a guy install sod at his new house and everyone drinks a bunch of beer afterward as their reward. I didn't know the man, but his wife was a friend of my sister Paula. I knew very few people there and didn't even have a beer. It was Sunday, a day to get over my hangover and chill out to get ready for the week ahead. After maybe an hour and a half of just sitting on the sofa and biding my time, I decided to head for home. I cruised through the east side of town on Route 17 going west toward the house when I got to the main north-south street, Schuyler Avenue. On a whim I decided to go into the Roundhouse Tap, where I had spent many nights with friends, just hanging out, talking and drinking. The bar was in an old downtown hotel. The Dale Carnegie Course had been held in one of the meeting rooms at the hotel. I'm not sure why I stopped at the Roundhouse that night. I had no intention of drinking. I guess I just wanted to see if anyone interesting was out that night.

As I walked past the bar, I looked straight ahead at a round table in the corner of the room. There sat the most beautiful redhead I'd ever laid my eyes upon. I couldn't believe what I was seeing. In a small town it's easy to think that you've probably met or at least seen everyone who might be worth considering for a romantic relationship. As my eyes gazed upon this beauty, I noticed a very close friend of my sister Mary was sitting with her. My heart began to race with anticipation of what I should do or say. I didn't even have a beer to calm me down. It was fight or flight time—I had to talk to this girl, one way or another.

Shelley Rivard was the woman my sister knew quite well. They went to elementary and high school together, and we had partied at my sister's apartment often on Friday nights. I once tried to seduce her back at St. Ambrose on a wild Saturday night, to no avail. Her brothers were friends with my brothers, and the family lived in one of those small West Kankakee homes that Uncle Pete had hauled sand to back before Azzarelli Construction got its start. Shelley and I were good friends, and I thank God she was sitting there at that moment. She got up, presumably to go to the restroom, and I went over to her and said, "Who is that redhead?" She replied, "Mary Benoit," and I calmly said, "Okay." Shelley went on her way. I went back to my spot near the bar feeling like a fool, still not knowing what to do or say. I almost left the place, but then Mary got up and started walking toward the bar—she was almost coming right at me! Seeing this made me almost shake to my soul; it was now or never. I touched her arm lightly and said, "You're Mary Benoit, aren't you?"

It was probably the greatest "line" I ever came up with, although I loathe that word—as though I needed a hook on the end of it to snag an unsuspecting woman. Saying meaningful things to attractive women has always been a source of fear and intimidation for me, as it is for many men. The prevailing mind-set is that these women have all kinds of guys at their beck and call, and you're just another one standing in line waiting to catch their fancy, so why bother?

Our conversation was short and went something like this:

"Yeah, I am. Who are you?" Mary said.

"I'm Jim Azzarelli."

"How did you know my name?"

"I've seen you around town here and there." *Yeah, right.* "Are you Ray J. Benoit's daughter?"

"No, I'm not. My dad is a farmer south of town by the fair-grounds."

"Well, how about me and you going out sometime?"

"Maybe."

"Could I get your phone number?" I asked.

"Let me go to the bar to get a beer and I'll write it down."

She came back in a few minutes and gave me her number. Soon after I left, knowing that I'd met someone special. I didn't care about hanging out. It was Sunday night, and I had to get going. Besides, I felt as if I'd done some great work that night. I played it cool for a couple of days, and then I called her and asked her out for that weekend. I took her to the Country Club. It was a very sterile place, but I had to meet my minimum food purchase requirements for the month there. We were both tense and it was obvious, but we made it through the small talk and actually started loosening up after a couple of beers. After that night I knew that I had fallen for Mary. I was in love with probably the best-looking girl in that small town. I hadn't seen her around because she went to a small, rural public high school south of town, Clifton Central, one of our football rivals. McNamara High kids didn't hang out much with Clifton kids. It was too far away and nobody knew anybody down there. She was all of nineteen, which explained why she hadn't been around much. She wasn't even the legal drinking age when I met her in that bar.

My newfound goal was trying to make her like me. I was concerned that my family name preceded me, and while that can be positive, it can also be a negative. Had she heard bad things about my family? Did she think I was arrogant? I realized that I couldn't really make anyone like me, and all I could do was just be myself.

I really wanted our relationship to grow, but I didn't want to come on too strong either. She lived in a tiny apartment on Station Street in West Kankakee, and after dinner each night I would go over to her apartment just to hang out with her. She was struggling with allergies because everything was in bloom at the time, so she wasn't going out much. I must have gone over there every night for two weeks. She had her hair in braids most nights—making her look like the Wendy's girl—and without make up she looked about fifteen or so, but I thought she was beautiful. About all I did on those visits was keep handing her Kleenex. She probably thought I was nuts, and I was nuts … for her.

I began asking Mary out on weekends. We did the usual bar scene, but it was different because I was with her. It was 1976 and disco was the rage. We would dance under the circling mirror ball to Kool & the Gang and other disco favorites. I started to feel the worm turn for me when one Sunday we went to church together. I saw Uncle Joe there and tried to tell her who he was, and she thought I was saying "Michael Joe." We both started giggling uncontrollably right there in God's house. I think He was smiling down on me that day. Later on we went to my cousin's college graduation day, and she met all of my family. She liked them. She was so friendly and outgoing. Mary was the perfect fit for me because we were so different but came from large families.

I got to go out to her dad's farm south of town and meet her family. She had five sisters and three brothers, but not all were living at home. I met her whole family at her brother Andy's high school graduation. They were all there in the school gym, and as Mary and I walked up those steps, I knew all those eyes were upon me. I felt quite intimidated, especially by her sisters, but they always made me feel welcomed. Her dad, Don, was just like Mary, outgoing and easy to be around. Being with her family really became fun; they would get together for anything and everything. They all loved to drink beer and laugh.

That summer we planned a trip to Chicago to see Paul McCartney & Wings. I arranged to have the Azzarelli company motor home that night to go to the concert. Someone had to be the designated driver, so I offered. I think Mary saw that as a sign of leadership and maturity. I didn't drink at all that night, and it didn't matter as long as I was with her. As we boarded the motor home, my cousin Nora climbed in and asked me who the new girl was. I replied, "Mary Benoit. She's the one!"

It was a great summer. I'd go to Mary's apartment after work, and we'd listen to Fleetwood Mac, Carly Simon, Art Garfunkel, Chicago, and Paul Simon. They became our favorite artists because we were falling in love and life was great. But something told me it was too good to be true. I began to doubt that I could really be in love—maybe I wasn't meant to have a long-term relationship. The old feeling that somehow I would undermine my own success started to creep in. I began to spiral into a depression of sorts and started doubting everything. I remembered the first "real love" experience I had a couple of years earlier, and that gnawed at me as well. Because of my doubts our relationship began to cool, and that made me doubt even more.

If I put my feelings and my soul out there, would I get hurt? Could I do this again—fall into that deep pit of dashed hopes and dreams for our future? This was the girl I'd been waiting for; it all seemed so right. I had held off having any serious relationships except for Linda, and that was a disaster. Because of my doubts, I was on the way to derailing my future with the right girl with whom I could share a long-term relationship and have a great family. Could it be done? It all sounded too romantic, too good, and I became somewhat overwhelmed by the situation.

One night at home I picked up one of my books from the Dale Carnegie Course, *How to Stop Worrying and Start Living!* I read it cover to cover and tried to do what it said: enjoy my life and stop fretting, neither of which will get the results I desired for my life. Just go after what you want and make it happen. Take it one day at time and enjoy life. That sounds so easy, but for me it never has been. I've struggled with almost every stage of life. Jethro Tull wrote "Nothing Is Easy" back in the early 1970s, and that has been an anthem for me. I figured, however, that if I could at least try to apply some of these concepts, maybe I could get past these desperate feelings of doubt I had in my soul. One motto I started to live by was, "Feel the fear and do it anyway." I started to consider the situation and began to realize it was time to move forward. Deep within me I knew I loved Mary, I felt I even had enough love in me for a whole family. That was huge, but I just had to somehow get past these feelings. I didn't really want to go back to the psychologist. I had Dale Carnegie to work with me.

Getting married to the right partner is just as important as picking the right profession. It's great to make a lot of money, but it's much better if you have someone with whom to enjoy it. If I were to make a lot of money but Mary and I didn't make it, my life would seem to be empty without her. I really wanted this to work. I just knew she was the one I wanted to live with forever. She had to feel the same way, though. I know things can go wrong in relationships, so that's why I became hesitant at this point.

One night turned things around. Mary and I went to a street party in downtown Bradley, a town connected to Kankakee in which my mother was raised. It was America's bicentennial, and we went with Mary's parents, Don and Barb. We had a great time, and her parents seemed so content with each other. They'd been married twenty-eight years or so, had nine kids, and were doing fine. Having nine kids has to be a tremendous challenge for two people. The teen years always complicate matters, as well as money issues and all manner of real life problems—let alone trying to keep a love relationship alive. But there they were, hanging out together, smiling and enjoying themselves, respected members of the community with nothing but high esteem for each other. Observing this made me start to look at my situation differently. If Mary came from this stock, there had to be something to her. I better not let her go and lose this opportunity; it may not come again.

When courting a mate, it's valid to consider that person's background and relationship with the family, especially the parents. It's important to find out what kind of people raised your potential mate. It may not be the biggest factor in your determination, but it is pertinent information to come to know and understand its implications. Mary came from solid stock, and she was very close to her parents and her siblings. She liked my family and I liked hers. Seeing her mom and dad that night did it for me. I knew then and there it was time to move forward in our relationship.

That August I asked her to marry me. It wasn't the traditional on-my-knees proposal. As we were leaving her apartment one evening, I said, "We ought to get married, you know?" She said something like, "Do ya think so?" I said, "Yeah," and she replied, "I'll think about it." We were so close by then that I didn't have too much doubt that she would say yes. Our dating lasted only four months—not much by today's standards. Couples often hang together for a year or two trying to figure out what to do, but not us. It was my time to set our destiny in motion.

Mary said yes the next morning, and she immediately went to work on the wedding plans with her mom. Charting my course destiny seemed pretty easy when I had only myself to consider, but now it was the two of us—a couple looking in the same direction with similar goals and attitudes about life. The most challenging part of our relationship was learning how to transfer my goals and aspirations from a single-minded orientation to include another person. Now it wasn't all about what I wanted to do; my plans had to include Mary. We set March 26, 1977, as our wedding date, and at that time it seemed to be way off in the distant future, but I've learned since that time moves in unpredictable ways.

Almost as soon as Mary said yes to my proposal, even greater doubts started to nag me. I started to wonder whether I had made the right decision. After all, we'd dated only four months. Was it too fast? All during those fall months I said nothing to Mary about those creeping doubts. She was always so upbeat that I didn't want to spoil the great karma we had created between each us. Outwardly, I cruised through the fall and into winter as if I were totally sure about everything.

Work in the late fall and winter months slowed down, and the regular road crews were laid off. I relegated myself to driving dump trucks, hauling stone from the quarries to the asphalt plant—a tedious task. The quarries were close to the plant, and the round-trips would take about half an hour. Driving that truck made me wonder, *How do these guys do this?* They drive a truck all day, every day, pushing that large mass of steel and rubber over the asphalt ribbon in continuous motion, only to have to downshift, upshift, and do it over and over again. I learned quickly that I wasn't suited for this part of the business, but it was better than sitting home, and most definitely better than laboring out in the cold. At least I could turn the heat on to warm my bones. By mid-November, it had already snowed and the great depression in my soul was on for the winter.

At night I would run to Mary, my refuge away from the cruel world of having to make a living. She would make me dinner many nights. I knew she was going to make a great wife and mother. I could see it in the way she treated me, cared for me, and was concerned with my thoughts and feelings.

CHAPTER FOURTEEN
Settling In

Driving the truck that winter was not the exciting job that I had thought it would be when I was a kid watching the trucks pass my house. Truckers are often taken for granted. Thousands of trucks roll up and down the road each day and we don't notice them, but they control the roads. Everyone races to pass them, dreading following behind them or sitting behind them at stoplights. They carry with them anywhere from fifty thousand to eighty thousand pounds, hauling asphalt, rock, dirt, or all manner of cargo. Trucking is a natural blues song—it's a lonely job, but, for the good of all, drivers make sure the load gets through only to get up the next day and do it all over again. In many ways it is a noble profession, but to me it felt more like insanity. At least there was a paycheck at the end of the week.

With the wedding drawing near, I began to feel like a slave to the paycheck. I had a very serious future to think about, one that would include a wife and children, so I figured I better keep hauling that stone to pay the bills. I never could get a handle on the truckers' life, but I knew this would be just a temporary gig, one that would only last a few months and disappear just as quickly as a winter Illinois sunset.

I did have my share of embarrassments in that dump truck. One time after I had picked up a load of stone at Lehigh Quarry, I parked my truck and went to the bathroom. Sitting on my throne I heard a loud *bam*! I thought it had to be some kind of an explosion, so as soon as I came out I asked someone, "What was that?" The guy looked at me flatly and said, "An Azzarelli truck just got hit by a train!" The sound of those words hit me like a punch to the stomach. There was my red tandem dump lying on its side with a freight car lodged up against it and stones all over the tracks. My heart went into my throat with fear, knowing that I, an Azzarelli, would not only get a royal ass chewing from my old man and my uncles, but I would be the subject of jokes and ridicule throughout the company for some time to come. And this is what happened. I was the butt of all truck driver jokes from then on.

Another time I was hauling stone and had gone to a job site, dumped a partial load, and then took off south down Rt. 50 just north of town. I passed a service station and noticed some guys staring at me. I wondered what they were looking at, so I looked back behind me to see my dump bed rising and dumping the rest of the load on the highway. I raced back to the job to get a loader to clean up the mess, hoping that no one would know what happened. Too late. As soon as I parked my truck at the end of the day, someone made a cocky comment about the incident and the joke was on me … again.

Maybe all this happened because of my attitude toward driving trucks, but I soon learned to hate driving all the more. I did learn to respect the safety factor, however. Driving a truck is nothing like driving a car. In addition to following numerous safety precautions, truck drivers have to go to great lengths to make sure everything goes right with the rig. Drivers are responsible for it—it's his livelihood and the company's property.

My Future Family

During this time I began to appreciate Mary more and more, especially, the way she was with her family. On Sundays we'd often go to the farm to see her parents. The farm was a typical lovely setting in rural Illinois, with expansive views of wide open prairie, and two barns, all situated a few miles south of Kankakee. Her dad, Don, had two shiny red GMC farm trucks to haul his grain, and he kept those trucks as clean as a young boy would keep a new bicycle. Everyone who knew Don Benoit liked him. He knew every farmer from Kankakee going south to Champaign and most of the ones going west to the Iowa border. He was a man's man and he loved life. One time, when I was at one of their many family functions, I was feeling somewhat out of place. Mary was off talking to her sisters, and I was just standing there alone. Don came over and said, "Come on, Jim Azz, let me get you a beer!" That's the kind of guy he was, always making me feel welcome and at home. I learned to love him. He was becoming a great friend, and he was going to be my father-in law.

The Benoit family had six girls and three boys. The boys tended to the tasks of helping their dad run the farm. The girls took care of the boys and the house. It was a classic Midwestern family-run farm, but Dad never let anyone in on what was going on with the nature of the business. That was typical of that generation; my dad and his brothers seemed to be cut from that same mold. Still, it was refreshing to see a tight-knit family, caring and loving each other and enjoying each other's presence. I came to love our trips out to that farm, as it reminded me of what was good and right about America, a hard-working farmer doing his thing, tilling out over a thousand acres each spring to raise the corn and beans in the blue-collar region of Central Illinois. This guy was a chain-smoking, let's-have-a-drink-after-work man who didn't believe in higher education. Most of the girls, except Julie and Denise, and all of the guys didn't even want to ask their dad to go to college. He thought it was better to get a job and not waste much time studying. Even Mary didn't want to go to college; she worked at Illinois Bell and made a decent living, so I figured with my pay and hers, we would live quite nicely.

Barb Benoit was a tough-love mother who practically raised the nine kids alone, since Don was out in the fields for long hours to bring home the bread to the family table. It takes a big heart and a lot of wisdom to raise nine kids out on a farm, and Barb has both of those qualities in abundance. She was a no-nonsense person who would always push the kids to be independent. She was a great cook, and those Sunday roast beef dinners were nothing short of spectacular. She always encouraged a person to eat beyond their limit. That Thanksgiving, we were caught between going to my folks or Mary's, so we decided to do both. After eating big at the Azzarellis', we went out to the Benoits'. I tried valiantly to act as though I was starving and had to force down more turkey and dressing. I didn't want to disappoint my future mother-in-law.

I observed how a family enterprise could work, as the sons worked directly for dad, interacting with him on a daily basis, learning from him and knowing what he expected from them. I could see the synergy between Don, Mark, Andy and Joe. I somewhat envied their relationship, being able to work with their dad every day. This would easily become a long-term business, a true family business. Don was a tough World War II Marine, but he was fair and good to work for, as the boys tended to the duties of the farm and made it all click. It reminded me of the way our family business had been built: the dad and sons living close together, working to build the enterprise that would grow into a multimillion-dollar business.

I began to see that in our business something was lost in the transfer from the World War II generation to my baby boomer generation. It was not a true family operation; it was more a large company that happened to be owned by blood brothers with the same last name. I was not sure how or if I would ever fit into this company.

The Wedding

Preparing for a wedding is like taking a trip into another dimension, as I found out that winter. I was getting married, but it was more like it was Mary's wedding and I just happened to be a participant in the proceedings. She and her mother made all the arrangements; I had virtually no input with any of the decisions. If I made a comment, it was received with comments such as, "Just show up on time and don't worry about it." But since wedding preparations are such a huge hassle, I didn't mind all that much. After all, her family was covering much of the bill, and I wanted her to have every special little effect she wanted in the ceremony and the reception. So I maintained my distance from all planning, and as long I did so we progressed with our relationship into the cold months of January and February.

The period of waiting and planning changed our relationship from being fun and airy to stiff and serious. The courtship period was a whirlwind of fun—spring and summer partying at the discos, finding great music together, and falling in love. Now, in the dark, dreary months of winter, I was on the verge of completely changing my life, and it was weighing upon me. Sure, there were doubts about it all, but I wasn't about to change anything. Mary handled it so much better than I, and I tried not to let on to my inner turmoil. Like my father, I've always been in inner turmoil, but I've tried to conceal it the best way I could—in relative silence and outer compliance. I could control it except for those moments when the inner frustrations bubbled over in the form of lashing out at someone over nothing. Mary learned in time to deal with my dual mentality of tenderness one moment and anger at the drop of a hat. Slowly, I began to learn when it was time to be controlled and when it was time to take control. I grew up in a family that thrived on some dysfunction, both within the confines of the home and at our place of business. At work it seemed no one got a pass on anything, especially the Azzarelli boys. We were often the object of anyone's ridicule, and I realized now that the abuse had taken its toll. Sometimes I would be in a dark mood and Mary would question why. I didn't have an answer besides, "That's just the way I am. Let's move on." I was always glad she could accept me for who I was.

The winter slowly turned toward spring, and the wedding was close at hand when my future brothers-in-law took me out on the town. I got buzzed, way more than usual, and somehow we ended up at the worst place for me to be like that—the Benoit family farm. I guess my language turned quite foul and things got a little crazy right in front of Barb. I woke up on the couch the next morning not knowing where I was and all I could think was, *Oh, no! What happened last night?* Jack Austin, who was married to Julie, Mary's sister, told me all the sordid details of me crawling around on the living room floor like a barking dog shouting expletives to Barb and her just laughing and taking it in. She gave me a pass, knowing it was my bachelor party, but I never intended for us to end up at the farm house. I thought I was in trouble, but she just had a few laughs at the breakfast table. I had a huge hangover, but I was glad to see that my future mother-in-law had no problem accepting me at my worst. It was another sign that I was marrying the right girl.

Finally, March 26, 1977, the day of our wedding, arrived. As far as March days in Illinois go it was a perfect ten—a sunny sky with temperatures in the low seventies. I made the decision to play golf that morning. Everyone was astonished to see me at the course, but I think it was a mute protest over the idea of being hooked up with someone else for life. I was the man of the house and would damn well do as I please! Just the fact that the weather cooperated made me feel that this was a good omen for me and Mary. We were most definitely in love and felt as if we were made for each other. While I had hidden much of myself from others, I had shown myself to her and she accepted me for who I am. That was the perfect combination—not being afraid to be myself and always feeling good about being around her even when things were not going so great. It all fit so well, and the wedding went off without a hitch.

The reception was and always is the best part of a wedding. The pressure is off and everyone can cut loose. We had a great time. Smitty was the best man and gave a great toast, but I don't remember anything he said. All of my dad's friends and political cronies were there, plus our golfing buddies and Mary's huge extended family. About six hundred people attended; it was the big event in Kankakee that spring. Mary and I stayed until the wee hours of the morning. Going back to her tiny apartment, our future home at least for a while, I had a real sense of gratitude to God—not just that the waiting was finally over, but that I had found *the* right person with whom to spend the rest of my life.

Newlyweds

The ensuing months were full of laughter for us in that tiny apartment, with its five hundred square feet. It being our first home made it all the more fun because it was the place where I had courted her and hung out with her during her sickest days of allergies and nasal congestion. All my feelings of uncertainty and foreboding about leaving behind my bachelor days had lifted. Living with Mary was easy, and we worked well together as a team. We rarely fought about anything except for my love to play golf every Saturday and Sunday during the spring and the summer. For me, it was a non-negotiable subject, but she was contributing significant money to the family budget. At the time I felt that I had to exert my dominance as a man and husband; after all, I was part Sicilian, and in that culture the male has dominance over the female. It was all so petty on my part, but I was trying to find my place in the relationship.

That spring my dad decided he would build us a home out in the country, a subdivision called Vaughndale where Dad had made a deal with a two farmers to develop the land and split the profits. The company mined all the stone from beneath the ground, used the stone for road construction projects, and turned the land into subdivided lots. Dad lined up the builder and did all the negotiations for the contract. His name was Ray Curl, a small-time builder but congenial guy. Dad always tried to get the bottom dollar price on everything, and Ray always relented. We moved into that house in August and were very happy to have some space to stretch out in, but we held onto our great memories of the apartment near the Dairy Queen on Station Street.

All that summer I worked as a foreman on the slurry seal crew, covering the streets of town with a tar-like sealer to cover the cracks for longer life. This was quite a challenge because, in the high humidity of the Midwest, the sealer takes a long time to cure, or dry out, and keeping traffic off the street was maddening. It was the first year the company had tried this venture, and I was the guinea pig. We lost money on many of the jobs, and I heard about it at the meetings. I tried to explain about the need for the flagmen to keep cars off the street, but it's tough to explain anything when it doesn't go well. So I just took it in stride and tried to learn from it.

At that time the uncles had decided to start letting us "kids" into their corporate meeting, and that seemed like a step in the right direction to me. I wanted to be part of the larger company and not just a field worker in the streets. It was interesting to hear the minutes of the last meeting and hear the uncles and dad discuss business. It was all fine until they started discussing us "kids"; that always seemed to turn into a haggle over who was to get this pickup truck or where someone would be working. Often tempers would rise as each uncle wanted to stake out their own son's turf within the business. It seemed things were growing apart among the brothers. I learned a lot about how I would *not* run a business at those meetings. However, I did pick up some knowledge in there as well.

The one aspect of being a part of the next generation that troubled me was that we always referred to as "kids." Maybe it was an endearing term to my dad and uncles, but I saw it as the sign that the transfer of power might never take place. I felt as if it were impossible to grow up, or just to grow as a person. Would I always just work on a crew, or would I be able to step and be a big-time executive and receive my birthright? Would I ever be treated as an up-and-coming person worthy of respect within the company and recognized as one of the future owners of the Azzarelli Construction Company? That idea seemed to be as distant as the next galaxy or maybe another universe entirely. The five brothers had their hands firmly on the wheel of this machine, and they weren't going to let go any time soon. Maybe never.

I had heard myths about how the first generation starts a business, the next one builds it up, and the third one tears it down. I'm not sure where that idea came from, but I think it was soundly engrained within all of their subconscious minds. The concept was usually told as a joke, but as a young impressionable guy, I took it to heart. How could I achieve my dreams and aspirations here, where, even at the lower levels of the pecking order, we were accorded virtually nothing in the way of respect? How would I ever make it to that promised land, the office where I could learn to plan out projects and have a say in the company's future? We were told that we would always have a job, but at this point that held no water whatsoever with me. I wanted to chart out a destiny of a much greater heights than running a slurry seal crew or driving a truck in the frigid climes of the Midwest. I felt trapped under the thumb of the World War II generation. We had good ideas also. We had abilities to manage, to learn, to excel. We could spread our wings as the brash baby boomer generation and carry on the tradition of excellence into the 1980s and beyond. But I was disillusioned with our prospects within the company. I figured they would have to let go someday, but how far out would that someday be—five, ten, or maybe even twenty years down the road?

At twenty-four, I was young, impatient, ambitious, and ready to take on the world. But there were chains around my feet and hands, and the world seemed small and inconsequential in that little town. I loved my new married life but had become disenchanted with working for a wage in a company that had probably peaked and would go nowhere without a fresh infusion of youth and new ideas. I knew we wouldn't be able to take over quickly, but I wanted confirmation that it would happen at some point.

Chapter Fifteen
A New Life

As the summer wore on, we settled into our new digs in Vaughndale. It was a brick, three-bedroom, two-bath ranch house with a fireplace and a redwood deck on the rear. Some might say it was the American dream, but a house and a ten thousand-square-foot lot were a lot less than what I considered to be my dream. The dream I wanted to pursue had more to do with self-actualization or, in my words, to realize my own capabilities, see them utilized to the fullest possible extent, and be rewarded accordingly. That's a lot more than money, but at my age, that would have meant a lot to me too. I wanted more of it and fast, but getting ahead was a slow process of working for the man in the construction business, even if that "man" was my father and uncles.

Everyone believed I had the perfect life because of my family's success. The truth, however, was that my life was quite ordinary with a lot of hard work and little acknowledgement of that work. I did have an extremely attractive wife who was good to me and for me. In that respect I had it pretty good. I was starting to realize that I had hit the jackpot with Mary. It must have been an answer to a prayer; in fact, some years later my mother said she prayed for me to find a good woman.

Once I saw a poster describing all the ingredients to success, and it said that marrying the right person is the key for about 90 percent of people who claim to be happy and successful. I agree. Mary and I had found that being together on a daily basis was really easy and comforting in its own right. Having status or position in the community was somewhat nice, but it would be quite empty without a compatible partner. One of my golfing buddies told me once that "you're claim to fame is your wife," which I never refuted and always felt proud about. Mary was not only my soul mate but my trophy wife. I was proud of the way other guys looked at her—she was mine and I loved it. After being married a while, we could sit for long periods of time without saying a thing, but saying it all. Non-verbal communication is a powerful force in a loving relationship. I never liked to argue or fight, and neither did Mary. We got along quite blissfully, as my earlier moodiness turned to contentment.

During the time Mary and I courted and married, a funny thing began to happen in Colorado. Nora had caught the eye of Steve Van Hook, and they fell for each other and made plans to be married in August 1976. This shocked me because I thought Steve (Tex) was a basic slug and wouldn't amount to much, but I was wrong—he was a tremendous slug. But he grew up a great deal and once he got a hold of a great woman like Nora, he became a man. Nora was everything he had dreamed of, but he couldn't get near her back in college because she and I were so close. We were almost kissin' cousins, as Nora would often say, because we clung to each other and our familial past. We were of the same Azzarelli mold and had been close since childhood. I was always grateful to Nora for leading me to Colorado State. Little did I know that while we were in the big house on Remington that Steve's heart beat loudly for her. I guess he suffered in silence for about a year until I left school, when he finally made his move—and he did it in a big way. They were married on August 21, and I was the best man. I had to give a toast in front of about

700 people, including introducing the governor of Illinois, Jim Thompson. At first I was intrigued that the governor would come to the wedding of Joe Azzarelli's daughter, but knowing Joe's political clout and involvement with various government projects, it was no surprise. It was nerve-racking to stand there with a microphone in my hand, talking to a room full of people, but my Dale Carnegie training helped me get through it just fine. The experience made me grow just a little bit. As Jerry Seinfeld said, public speaking is most people's number one fear, with death being second, which means that most people would rather be in the coffin than have to give the eulogy.

Later that summer and into fall I moved over to the asphalt crew and grabbed a shovel and helped out the best I could. Little did I know at the time how big of a role that asphalt paving would become in my future. I loved being on big road jobs, laying the hot mix that thousands of vehicles would pass over each day. It was very productive and fast money, even though no one ever let us "kids" see the company's books (they were kept in a secret place where no one could see them for fear of knowing too much). Being outdoors was great. In many ways, I liked the outdoor work better than being indoors, but I knew that somehow I had to get on the inside of the company.

That fall Mary and I made a trip to Notre Dame for a great weekend of partying and football. We met Smitty and Chris over at South Bend to see the Fighting Irish beat Alabama 10-0 on a sunny Saturday afternoon in November. It brought back some good memories of the weekends we had there back in our college days. The memories were great, but I didn't miss college that much. Since I'd gotten married, I felt that I was on my way—headed somewhere, even though I wasn't quite sure of the destination. But that was about to change.

ONE LAST WINTER

December had to be one of the coldest months in history. We got more than two feet of snow and had a drift that reached the top of our garage. At one point, the wind chill went down to fifty degrees below zero. Even with the heat going full blast and a fire in our fireplace, the warmest we could get the temperature in the house was fifty-eight degrees. I complained to Dad about it, and when I went into the upstairs storage area, I discovered that Ray Curl had left out 90 percent of the insulation. Old Ray apparently got back at Sam for beating him down on all the prices on the house. We all learned that no matter how good a price we're looking for, the other guy has to make a living as well.

Just facing another winter was almost more than I could stand. I went back to driving trucks, but the weather was so bad there was very little work to do. I was stuck at home for several days at a time and I wanted to climb the walls from cabin fever. Then, one day a couple of weeks before Christmas, Uncle Joe held a fateful meeting that changed my life.

The company had slowed to a crawl because of lack of work and the weather stalling any projects they could muster. When Joe saw that the company was accumulating more family in the business, he wanted to unload some of the boomer generation. At the meeting he said, "We have too much overhead here. Does anyone want to move to Florida?" I couldn't believe my ears. It was like someone opened up a window of sunshine and happiness, one which subconsciously I had been waiting for since I was eleven years old and Dad had taken me to Florida. It was February back then, and when I stepped off the plane and felt the seventy-degree weather, I thought, *This is where I want to live.* That was part of a dream that I had envisioned for so long that a great joy filled my heart. I knew this was my chance to make a new and great life for me and Mary and our future children. I thought of all the new possibilities and great opportunities that Florida might hold and the chance that one day there would be self-actualization of some sort. In Florida I would find an atmosphere much more conducive for establishing my talents, the ones I knew were latent inside me just waiting to explode out of my shell of inhibitions.

I raised my hand and said eagerly, "I'll go." Surprisingly, I was the only young guy in that room who had the inkling to move. Everyone else either had a kid or two or just wanted to stay in the area of their birth. My brother Rick didn't want to go because he was in love with his future wife, Vicki. At the time, I really wished he would go so we could face life in Florida together. Later, after he got married, he did move to Florida, but I'm not sure if he really wanted to move or was just pleasing Uncle Joe to lighten the company load. After the meeting I had a good talk with Uncle Pete about the possibilities down in Tampa, and we talked about my going to work at Delta Asphalt, the company formed by our family, J. W. Conner, and Jim Walter. I was elated at the prospect of working outside the family but still being connected in another aspect of the family business. I also liked the idea of learning all I could about the paving business.

My window of opportunity was clearly in front of me, and it was wide open.

MOVING TO FLORIDA

I had only one hurdle to clear: I had to tell Mary we were moving. I was so excited that I didn't even tell my Uncle Joe that I'd have to discuss it with my wife, and now I was afraid she might object to going. I felt guilty about not consulting with her first, but it all happened so fast. As soon as I told Mary, she immediately started crying about leaving her family. I tried my best to paint a picture about how great our future would be in the Sunshine State and away from the dreary Illinois. In the end, it wasn't that tough of a sale. When Mary called her mother and told her about the situation and how bad she felt about leaving the family, the farm, and her life here, Barb told Mary, "You go where your husband goes." This spoke volumes, and soon Mary began to accept the idea and started looking forward to the move as much as I was.

I had traveled so extensively that I was mentally prepared to make the move. I had seen so much of the world beyond Illinois that I knew there were places out there nicer (at least for me) than the cornfields of the Midwest. On a visit back to Illinois after we had moved, a good friend said, "There's no place like God's country," meaning the Midwest. That's true in a way, but I had seen so many people not go to new places out of fear. The great unknown often conjures up angst and concern, but I had been to Florida many times over the years and I knew I had a job there, so my fears were minimal.

That winter was the first one I could remember where I hadn't felt the blues. The colder it got, the happier I became just knowing I would soon to leave. We set early February as our moving date, which meant I would miss more of winter. The winds blew hard that January, but inside of me was a southern fever. I was ready to explore the next phase of my life in a new place full of promise and vitality. The cold days couldn't drag me down anymore. My attitude toward life had transcended the wintertime sadness that had pervaded my soul for so long. There was no doubt in my mind that I was doing the right thing not only for myself, but also for my wife and the children we would someday have. Leaving the Midwest would hold no sadness for me, but I tried to be somewhat understanding for Mary, for she had never known anything different. I knew it would be an adjustment for both of us. Change is never easy and can be stressful for a newly married couple. However, I told myself that moving away could bring us closer together as a couple. That would prove true.

I see now how my willingness and desire to move was similar in many ways to Grandfather Nanu's fateful move from Sicily.

Nanu wanted to move due to the impoverished conditions he experienced in Sicily and desperately wanted to seek a chance to better himself in the new world. He was stepping out on a limb, but he probably didn't feel as though he had much to lose. The hard part for him and Nana, of course, was leaving the family behind. But he knew that if he was given a chance, with his work ethic he could overcome any hardship.

Having family around comforts the soul and makes us feel connected to something important, something permanent. It gives us a sense of grounding—there's always someone to care for us and love us. For Nanu, leaving his family in Italy was a major concern. Leaving family behind in those days was almost like a death, because there was no jumping on planes to see the folks in Sicily for a couple of weeks. The separation had to be excruciating to both him and Nana because they knew they might never see their parents again. That is one sacrifice that we, as third-generation Americans, can never fully appreciate, but we can be eternally grateful for it. In the film *Godfather II*, there is a scene at the playhouse where the immigrant in New York gets word from the Old Country that his momma has died. The poor man is totally devastated by the news—Momma is dead, and he's all the way over here on the other side of the planet in America. How many times did this scene play out in the lives of immigrants? A great many, of course, but that was their sacrifice to get to the New World, the land of opportunity. The guilt they felt must have been overwhelming, knowing deep inside that they had forsaken their families for a "better" life. But their roots went back to the homeland, where their parents raised them to be upstanding people. The drive to create this "better" life had to be an overriding factor, pushing them, driving them past their fears, and especially moving them past the enormous pull of the heart strings and the love of family.

This willingness to move far away from the family proves that Maslow was on to something in his hierarchy of needs theory. In the deficiency stages of existence there is a need for security of employment, revenue and resources. This is second lowest part of the pyramid; the first is the basic needs, such as the need to breathe, sleep, and eat. Being in those impoverished conditions, Nanu knew he had to do something dramatic to break out, so he moved away, forever. With that, he and millions of other immigrants of varying ethic backgrounds brought forth a new, vibrant energy and work ethic that would eventually explode into a new America. The country was poised for growth and fueled with a new momentum that would carry it forth through the twentieth century and up to today. The sacrifices made by those immigrants are this country's economic foundation— built through hard work, innovation, and production of goods and services.

My moving to Florida had much to do with the same hierarchy of needs. I was frustrated working for the company in Illinois, feeling trapped and not seeing things getting any better in the near future. In the hierarchy there is a need for esteem, and I was lacking this in my situation up north. Working all the different jobs there was okay, but I had a distinct feeling that we, as the next generation, would not get a shot at the top rungs of the ladder of the corporation, even though we were Azzarellis and our dads owned the company. I also felt underappreciated because of my carelessness driving a truck, and I became the butt of many jokes within the company for a brief time.

In the hierarchy of needs there is a need for self-respect and respect from others. I had neither at the time. In fact, I felt complete disrespect coming from my co-workers in the field. Any little mistake was accentuated and ridiculed to the point where I found myself wanting to lash out at others or simply go into a funk. My basic needs were met because my job was secure and I had a great wife, but the need for esteem and self-actualization were not. I had to move on to a new scene. Yet, my low self-esteem gnawed at me and made me wonder if I was making the right decision … again. Second-guessing myself would lead to many a sleepless night. However, once

I made a decision, especially a big one, I always stuck to it. The key to making good decisions is to go with my instincts even though I might have doubts. Everyone has doubts, but if you can listen to other opinions and then decide what you need to do, you can move forward in confidence. Once you've done that, go with your gut and move on. It may sometimes feels like a free fall from an airplane, not knowing whether the parachute is going to open, but that's part of the excitement of the ride.

CHAPTER SIXTEEN

The Times, They Are A-Changin'

Having the right mate is the key to handling change. And moving toward the ultimate goal of self-actualization, the highest point of the pyramid of needs, requires the support of the right person at home. You have to know that your spouse loves you and will walk with you through the fire. I have felt that way about Mary since we first started dating. When everything around me went crazy, she was always the one waiting for me after work with a kiss and a hot meal. Without her at my side, I'm not sure I could have made the move to Florida, and I might have remained stuck at the lower part of the pyramid for my entire life.

I have always had a sense of an inner passion or a guiding of the spirit inside me. I remember as a grade school kid talking to my friends about what my dreams were. I knew I wanted four kids—two girls and two boys—and this has come to pass. I also knew that someday I wanted to be my own boss, and this also came to be. Henry David Thoreau wrote in *Walden*, "... if one advances confidently in the direction of his dreams, and endeavors to live the life which he has imagined, he will meet with a success unexpected in common hours." This has always been a favorite of mine because, even in the face of great doubt, I've been able to move toward a better situation without letting fear overtake me.

Leaving my and Mary's family behind in Illinois was difficult, especially for Mary. I was close to my family as well, but I had been away at college for four and a half years and had become used to it. Mary had traveled very little and had never been separated from her family for more than a week or two. Facing this upcoming separation no doubt caused her anxiety about what was to be. I figured she would like Florida, but how could I know? What if she didn't? I did not want to consider that alternative, the possibility of moving back (although that almost did occur later on in the early 1990s). The situation in my work up north was not bad such as Nanu's economic depravation, but I had an emotional depravation— a lack of respect from others and even my own self-respect. I craved this desperately, so I had to leave to search for the greener pastures of the Sunshine State. I didn't know what may lie ahead, but I knew with my work ethic and my optimism about Tampa, it had to be better than what would happen in the company in Kankakee.

Similar to the immigrants moving to America in the early 1900s, people were flocking to Florida at the rate of approximately one thousand per day during the 1980s and '90s, creating a boom which elevated Florida to the fourth-most populated state. The land rush of Florida was on, and I was thrilled to have a chance to stake my claim, just like the pioneers did back in the wild west.

The spirit of the pioneer sees life as a vision of the future, a future filled with happiness and great expectation. I think this spirit is akin to the Holy Spirit to the Christian, which I believe is true in my case. But to the non-Christian, it might be the human spirit, the force giving the person the willingness to look beyond what is and ask, "What are the possibilities?" It's a restless spirit that can't sit still and must keep moving. We as pioneers, immigrants, or just plain go-getters have an idea that something is out there for us and we have to go see if we can get it. The trick is to harness this energy into a positive force that will lead to something productive and useful for yourself and your family. In my case I had to tell Mary to strap it down and enjoy the ride. I didn't know if we were headed to fortune or total destruction. While most folks are looking to conform to their peers and not make too many waves, the pioneer wonders just how many waves are there and just how large they become. The pioneer sees life as an adventure; it's just too damned boring working that nine-to-five job in the office. In a sense, uncertainty is what the self-reliant thrive on—what will happen next? How will I react in this situation? It's testing the upper limits of not only the fear of failure but also your imagination to get through "pickles" of your own devise.

The fear of failure is always present inside of us, and we are never comforted by success because we all know failure is just as common as success. Conversely, failure can be turned into success. You don't know if your success will last, or how long. You have to learn how to ride it as a surfer rides a wave, just trying to balance and stay on your feet as long as possible. The trick is to not to allow any failure to stamp itself on your self-image. You need to view every failure as an experience that you can learn and profit from and realize that another chance will most assuredly arise in the future as long as you keep moving toward your destination. Sometimes, you may realize there is no clear destination because you have achieved all your previous goals. That's when the true pioneer sets new goals and adopts a new purpose. *Retirement* is not in the pioneer's vocabulary. There is little rest for a free spirit— only new horizons to see and new mountains to climb. This spirit made America grow, and it was born in me. I know I am a chip off Nanu's block.

In moving to Florida I had to come to grips with one fact—my dreams of being an owner in Azzarelli Construction Company were over. I was leaving the main office of the company and going to an outside company, Delta Asphalt in Tampa. Even though we had a one-third ownership interest in Delta, I knew this was the end for my life with Azzarelli. Azzarelli Construction in Tampa was run by my two uncles, Bart and Pete, and I knew beyond a doubt that I would never work for them. They had plenty of family there and didn't need anymore. I was hopefully setting myself up to someday run Delta, but that was not the same as being an executive with Azzarelli.

With this realization came some sense of sorrow, because for some time I had felt this was my birthright, something I would enjoy and cherish the rest of my life. Not only would I be able to enjoy all the trappings of being an owner of a respected firm in town, but I felt this was part of Nanu's vision. But was it? Did he really see anything beyond the brothers' coming out of poverty and into local and state prominence? I'm not sure he had any deeper visions than simply moving the family out of destitution, and it panned out very well for all of them. I wanted to believe that he did see something in it for me and my cousins, but now I'm not so sure. I had wanted the next generation to take charge and show what we could do.

In leaving the Midwest, I was leaving everything I knew and loved, including my family, Mary's family, and many friends and golfing buddies. At times I felt bitterness toward the ones who wouldn't allow our generation to take a larger role in the business, but that didn't get me anywhere. My gleeful attitude toward moving seemed to belie my true sense of loss: My name is Azzarelli, the name on all the dump trucks racing through our city, and I had always been so proud of that fact. I figured we would be in charge one day. We would have the helm of the ship, and we'd all make a ton of money together. However, as Pink Floyd said, "the child has grown, the dream is gone."

It was sad leaving my childhood paradise, Spaghetti Hill, the familiar town, the big city, where we had gone to so many Sox games and concerts, and of course our beloved country club, where I learned how to play golf. Part of life is dying to something that's so familiar only to be born into a new life, where so many new experiences push you, stretch you, and make you a new person. So many people I know are still back in Kankakee living in their parents' homes and still in the same jobs. So many of them avoided change. Not that it's all bad for them—that's just the way they wanted it, or at least I suppose they did. I wonder how many would have loved to have left and pursued other dreams.

In many ways, it is easier to grab on to anything that feels like security, such as a job, even though creatively it may be a dead end. Staying in a job without the hope of fully using and developing your God-given abilities often means sacrificing the great joys and satisfactions of doing it on your own or being your own man. Not everyone can accomplish this in their lives. Not everyone can own their own business or become a great athlete or a success in the entertainment business or the arts. On the other hand, many people settle for a career path that is something less than what they could achieve. Often we must give up on the life we may have dreamed of as a child or young adult, but we should give up on those dreams only after we have tried everything within our power to make them happen and when we are positive that we would be happier settling for something else and being free of the burden of pursuing them.

To search for any kind of real and lasting security simply does not work because nothing stays the same. For example, that's why the Social Security program doesn't work. It was supposed to assure Americans that everything would be all right when we retire, but there was no mechanism for it to grow and change with inflation, so almost no one can afford to retire on his Social Security income alone. It proves the truth that if you fail to plan ahead, you are doomed to fail.

Another disillusionment the American people have to reckon with are the attitudes of the modern corporation. In previous generations, people could always count on a steady job with incremental pay raises and a nice pension at retirement. That paradigm has completely changed over the years. Today's worker must be careful not to price himself out of a job. Be careful as you get those raises, or you may wind up losing your job to someone younger and less costly, even though you've got more tenure and experience. The global economy has resulted in large companies going out of the country for cheap labor in places like India, the Philippines, and Mexico. Consequently, our labor force has had to adjust to sweeping changes, and the American Dream has had to be altered in the process. However, Americans are a resilient bunch, and we will find a way to keep our great economy thriving even if both spouses have to work, which is now the standard, or even if some men have to take two jobs just to keep the dream alive.

Americans will always survive because we subscribe to the "whatever it takes" mentality, an attitude that has been handed down to us through the generations. That doesn't mean there isn't a long-term cost. Part of the fallout from this situation is evident in our rising divorce rate, which now is at 60 percent. Families who might have made it together before are now splitting up, separating children from their parents. We're becoming a nation of single mothers raising kids who see their fathers every other weekend.

Often, compromises must be made to reach for the brass ring. My idea of the American Dream included Mary staying at home with the kids, but it has been a balancing act for us. Without her working, it became harder to reach my financial goals. I was impatient to get rich, but at least our move to Florida put an end to our fighting over the country club bill, because there was no way we could afford to join one in Tampa.

Moving South at Last

Finally, February 5 came, and it was time to pack up our two cars and roll south. It was a frigid, twenty-degree morning when we stopped at the McDonald's on East Court St. in Kankakee. We got our Egg McMuffins and coffee, and Mary, my brother Rick, and I were more than ready to roll down I-57 toward our new home. At the time CB radios were popular, so we used those to keep in contact with each other. The barren trees and low sun reminded me why I was leaving Illinois.

As we pulled out onto the interstate, I could feel the surge of adrenaline carry me down the road. It was the satisfaction of knowing I had found the right woman and the certainty of moving to Florida. We spent two full days on that road, and it was exhilarating. We were on our way to a whole new life.

As we drove across the Florida state line, I could sense the great expectations of things to come. Working in a new company outside the Azzarelli family frightened me somewhat but excited me as well. Ironically, when we arrived the weather in Tampa was cold by Florida standards. The high for the first month there each day was about 55 degrees, and this was somewhat disappointing. We had bought a house about three miles north of Tampa Stadium, where the Buccaneers play their games. It was a small, three-bedroom, two-bath stucco home with a fireplace. I never thought we'd need the fireplace in Florida—how wrong I was. The first night staying in that chilly house I suffered a near a panic attack. As the sun went down, the dark settled in and it seemed to seep into my heart. As we lay there in bed, I started crying, and so did Mary. We couldn't believe we had finally made the move. The cold, hard reality of being on our own set in, and establishing ourselves in a new environment seemed like a staggering hill to climb. It wasn't so much that I wondered whether or not I'd made the right decision. It was more being overwhelmed by the enormity of turning our lives upside down and moving out of the comfort zone of our safe hometown and familiar surroundings. We had taken the chance; now we were about to find out if it would pay off.

Chapter Seventeen
The American Dream

I had set out to find the American Dream. I was in search of that intangible concept we all are looking for, the ideal that, like an open highway in the desert, will take us to somewhere far better than where we are today. What is it really? I don't know exactly, but each of us fun-loving baby boomers has his own concept of it. Most likely that concept involves the acquiring of wealth in one way or another. At twenty-four years old, my idea of the American Dream was having it all—a great wife, a nice, big home, four kids, plenty of money in the bank, and being able to travel to exotic places at will. I saw my dad and his brothers do it; now it was my turn to grab for the big dream. I even dreamed of having a private jet and owning all kinds of income-producing real estate that would ultimately make me a multimillionaire. Seeing all the growth around me in Tampa made me realize that anything was possible here. It was the new American frontier, a place where dreams could thrive, a state exploding with "immigrants" from other parts of the country searching for the same fresh start.

Unfortunately, my hang-ups followed me. Moving from Illinois to Florida did not cure me of my doubts and fear of failure. My failures as a son of a boss were still there—not fulfilling what I thought was my birthright, feeling like I was the butt of so many jokes within the company. These were still fresh upon my mind as I prepared to go to work for Delta Asphalt Paving Co. of Tampa.

The New Job

Going to work at Delta was an eye-opening experience. The first day I showed up at the plant, Charles Ramsey, the general manager, asked me where I wanted to work in the company. I was taken aback by this question; I didn't anticipate being able to make my own call as to what part of the company I would toil in. I think Charles was a bit intimidated by Uncle Pete, because Pete had that effect on many people, Even though my family owned part of Delta, I wanted to start from scratch and prove my worth to others and to myself. I surprised Charles when I told him I wanted to work on an asphalt crew with the laborers and learn how to run a paving machine. Delta offered me clerical uniforms, and that rankled me. I was a worker, not an officer, but I reluctantly took them anyway. I think the general manager held my family in high esteem due to our ownership in the company and thus wanted me to keep the uniforms. In retrospect, I realized that I had a slave mentality—I was meant to work out in the hot sun for an hourly wage. I couldn't make it in business; that was for my uncles and smarter guys than me. What if I didn't learn the office work or wasn't accepted by the people at Delta? Would I feel like a failure?

I went to work the next day on a paving crew consisting of one white foreman and six black guys, two white workers, and a Cuban guy named Roberto. When they found out who I was, they were all stone-cold and couldn't believe I would be out there sweating on the steamy pavement. Little did I anticipate how much effect the Azzarelli name had on them. I felt all eyes were upon me as I tried to make friends with the crew. It was probably the weirdest feeling I've ever had in the workplace, their knowing I was kin to the owners of the company. I was put on a pedestal yet hated at the same time out of sheer jealousy. It was like I had traded being the joke of the company for being the rock star of the company. I didn't want to be either one; I just wanted to work and learn from the ground up. The foreman, Carl Tapley, kept a close eye on me. I think he figured I was there to keep an eye on him. He had a reputation as an alcoholic. Everyone said he kept booze in the truck. Some of the guys thought I was there to take over the company from Charles Ramsey. Whatever the case, I created quite a buzz among the forty or so employees of the business. For my part, I just tried to fit in with the crew as best as possible for the first few months—playing dice in the back of the crew truck with the guys from Lakeland, the blacks who drove the forty-two-mile drive each day because of the lack of skilled paving workers in Tampa.

It was as if I were royalty coming out of my castle to live with the peasants, trying to be one of them. They didn't know I had been accustomed to this kind of labor. It was no big deal to me, but it certainly was to them. I always felt as if there was a cloud of suspicion surrounding me at work. It was not comfortable at all, but I dealt with it as best as I could, knowing that one day I would hopefully rise from the ashes of the slave mentality that dogged me since my early working days. Being the object of jealousy is a tough grind to dig out of. It's not easy for me just to stick my nose up and adopt a "just deal with it" attitude. I wanted everyone to like me, but I soon began to realize that no matter what I did or said, the grudge many co-workers had against me would not go away anytime soon. Later on, I found out that most of the workers over at the Azzarelli Company in Tampa thought that all of us boys received a million dollars when we turned twenty-one. That was so far from the truth. Now, my cousin Mike was quite the flashy bachelor, driving a 450SL Mercedes con-vertible, living in a posh apartment, and flying the company helicopter. Understandably, this led many to believe we were all quite affluent.

Everyone wondered why I moved to work at Delta, a mere satellite company of three large companies. I explained that I was trying to get away from my family business, but that was hard for them to understand. I was supposed to have been born with a silver spoon in my mouth, and I should be riding on the gravy train with the rest of my cousins. It made me sometimes question my own reasons for working there, but looking around at the green grass and palm trees, I knew at least I was in a better place. When working with the crew, I got no hassles from management. A major scandal was unfolding at the time of my arrival, however. Upper management reportedly had been "doing jobs on the side" and collecting cash for their own pockets and not putting it back into the company. Delta was a prime target for such a scandal because none of the three principal companies had a representative at the plant or any of the job sites. No one was minding the store, and if the door is left open, someone will undoubtedly walk in and take what he pleases. At the time everyone suspected Charles was the culprit, but it was never proved and there was no formal investigation into the matter.

After about three months, Charles told me he wanted me to come into the office and learn how to estimate paving jobs. It was music to my ears, as I was tired of being in the hot sun day in and day out. I thought my work would become more interesting and stimulating, but storm clouds were brewing on the horizon.

A Family of My Own

Soon after starting my new job, we learned that Mary was pregnant with our first child. We hadn't been married for a year, but we thought it was time to start the family we had talked about so much. I was thrilled, of course, because this was another step in my fulfilling my destiny. Why is it that having kids is so much a part of the American Dream? You'd think we'd want to keep all the money we can gather and just enjoy it. Not true. We want to extend ourselves to future generations. Maybe it stems from a desire to become "immortal," passing part of ourselves on to future generations and sharing what we have as a couple with others, our own flesh and blood. The alternative seems like selfishness, keeping it all for ourselves. The truth is that raising children probably produces more joy than anything else we do. The duty of raising children can be extremely trying, but it's also very rewarding. Often I hear people talk with disdain about raising their kids—"getting them grown up and out of the house." Those people are missing the fun in it all. They were there through it all but failed to enjoy it one day at a time, one little challenge after another, until they have grown up and left like a wispy breeze on a clear day—leaving behind only the memories and the occasional visit or phone call.

Looking forward to our first baby helped me face my challenges at work. Mary was adjusting nicely to our new neighborhood, Lago Vista. She began to meet many of the neighbors and soon they became friends. I've always said, "Everybody loves Mary, and so do I." It was true. She took to our new town gracefully, getting to know many people rather quickly, especially Marilyn Salling, who would become her Florida "mother." Marilyn was a sweet lady with a lovely southern accent who became a close confidante of Mary's through that first pregnancy. Our loneliness and separation anxiety from our Illinois families began to fade as we assimilated into the swelling sea of the Florida's immigrants. There were so many people there from somewhere else that we were all in the same boat.

WEARING THE WHITE COLLAR

My estimator mentor was Richard Courbat, a huge man of almost four hundred pounds who endured a serious asphalt plant accident that severed his foot. Surgeons reattached the foot, but Richard was in constant pain. When I met Richard, he was a very sensitive, insecure guy with a distinct fear of ridicule and being fired. After I knew him a while, he told me that the first day I showed up he told his wife he may have to seek employment elsewhere because an Azzarelli was here to replace him. I was glad to work under Richard because, despite his worry about his job, he tried to teach me all he could about estimating asphalt projects. It was a refreshing change from my days at Azzarelli up north.

Unfortunately, the other players in the office—the dispatcher, the front desk girl, the plant foreman, and the asphalt quality control man—all seemed to have the "I hate Azzarellis" syndrome. The look Luther Ellis, the quality control man, would give me every time I asked a question was nothing short of vile, so much so that I avoided him as much as possible. My appearance in the office represented a threat to some people and was painful to others. Their small minds tried to figure out why any family member of the owners of the company would want to work there and snoop on them. The movie the *Big Chill* had not been released by then, but it would have fit the description of how I felt being employed those first six months at Delta. Going from the joke of the company up north to the new rich kid in town made me feel that there was no escape from my "fame" as an Azzarelli. I could only imagine the kind of envy, scorn, and rude treatment that really famous people sometimes experience from others. Most of it is dished out by small people who think you're less than human because you have money. The truth was, I didn't have money. Everyone assumed I did. I just happened to have the last name "Azzarelli," which I was proud of nonetheless.

Only about a week had gone by in my tenure in the office when Charles Ramsey was suddenly gone. No explanation was given. We felt like sheep without a shepherd. Rumors started to fly about our new manager, who had previously had the helm at Delta. His name was Jimmy Conner, and Richard used to call him "Captain Morte." I soon found out why. Jimmy came from the J. W. Conner clan of construction hard knocks and had an air of both arrogance and depression. He was tougher than nails, never smiling at anyone, especially at work. He was a chain-smoking alcoholic brought up by a never-can-please father. Just seeing Jimmy the first time sent chills throughout my body, and I knew I would be in for a very long haul with this tough guy. He immediately let me know in no uncertain terms that this was to be no gravy train for me. I felt the searing sting of bitterness coming from the core of his being. Even his look would send my heart into panic attacks that made me wonder, *What did I get myself into? Am I at the wrong place at the wrong time? Who the heck made this guy king?* Each day I was afraid to go to work, not knowing what to expect from this hyper-volatile king of the hill. I seriously began to consider going over to work with Uncle Pete and Uncle Bart at Azzarelli in Tampa, so you *know* I was suffering.

However, I decided to stay and fight through my terror of having to work for this maniac, dealing with the daily rant-ing and ravings over some things I considered absurd. I often wondered if this guy would ever chill out. I felt like he was out to get me, and at times he did have me. I felt like his prey.

My self-esteem sunk to a new low working under Jimmy. I figured he hated the Azzarellis as bad as everyone else in that company. I began to feel trapped in a web of jealousy and ha-tred from others plus my own fear, which had a stranglehold over me. I even had bad dreams about working under him. He seemed to be ever present, with no way of getting away from him. My Florida dream seemed to be crumbling beneath me before I could realize it.

For a while Jimmy had me doing odd jobs, such as carrying tools to the crews or running menial errands for the office personnel. Then one day Jimmy sent me to a traffic control workshop. Then he sent me to another one and then an occasional seminar. I began to get the idea that he thought more of me than just a "gofer." One week he put me to work in the asphalt plant, loading trucks with hot asphalt so that I could get some experience in that part of the business. Then he began to teach me the basics of blueprint reading, which came in handy later. Of course, in the presence of the other employees, he still would not show me any respect or courtesy for fear of them thinking that he favored me because of my last name. He treated me like crap, which gave me ambivalent feelings as to what he was up to—one day I felt like I was on the move; the next day I was at the bottom of the dung pile. It was up and down, but gradually getting better. And then disaster struck.

During a six-week period we had a string of backing accidents by some of the dump truck drivers. This really upset Jimmy, and during our monthly safety meeting he gave a dissertation about the problem with these accidents. "The next person that has a backing accident will be fired," he announced. About a week later we were doing some paving out at Tampa International Airport, and I was there watching the crew pave. I hopped into my bright yellow pickup and proceeded to back up … and smashed right into Jimmy's car! I sat there in my truck dumbfounded, fearing the consequences. How could I have done that? All the idiotic things I had done back up north came rushing into my mind. All that I wanted to escape, my wanting a fresh start, my aspirations for a better life at work all came crashing down in that single moment. I was a laughingstock of the company—again. Everyone on the crew stared at the whole scene in utter astonishment. They couldn't believe what had just transpired, and neither could I.

I grimly drove back to the office. Jimmy was not far behind. He had me come in his office and fired me on the spot. I got fired from my own family's company! I use to think that was an impossibility. It simply could not happen unless I was being a total jerk, unwilling to work or produce anything at all, which I never was. I always wanted to learn and grow. But it was not to be. I was fired. What an awful feeling. What would the family think? What would my wife think? I had to get a job elsewhere. I had worked for someone other than the family for only a few short weeks back in college. Besides, I liked the paving business and felt my best chance to progress was at Delta.

I had to do some serious self-assessment. Was I taking myself too seriously? Was I just a big screwup? Did my aspirations exceed my abilities? What was wrong with me? What was right with me? Was it some kind of subconscious hatred for Jimmy that made me run into that car? I replayed that event for many days in my mind, and I came to one conclusion. I had put him in an untenable position through that accident. It was a stupid accident, and somehow I had to move on and get my job back. I called Jimmy.

I sucked up my pride and asked him if we could meet for coffee. We did one night, and I apologized for the accident. I knew it put him in a bad position in front of the employees, and I told him I would adjust my attitude toward him and everyone else at the company. Being in a position of entitle-ment, I had to take a hard look at my complacency. Maybe my attitude was a problem. Maybe I thought I had a guaran-teed job and that being an Azzarelli gave me some privileges above others. I didn't think I was doing that, but maybe it was a factor. I told Jimmy that I thought it was partly my attitude and partly his disposition all rolled into one ugly mess. I was very contrite about the whole situation. My fate was in his hands.

I think Jimmy was amused by the whole situation. It was well known that he had been the black sheep of the Conner clan, on the outside looking into the contracting empire the Con-ner family had created in Tampa. His cousin J. W. Conner and Pete Azzarelli were the high-rolling tycoons calling the shots in the contracting arena of Tampa and presided over the Azzarelli-Conner-Delta business deals. He had Pete's nephew on the ropes, and I'm sure it gave him some satisfaction, as he resented Pete a lot. He had even told me so. I'm sure that he had dealt with plenty of insecurities within himself growing up with a verbally abusive father who also had been in the construction business, one of the original Conners who helped build Alligator Alley, the road that connected the west coast of Florida to the east coast, spanning the treacherous Everglades in the process. It was quite an engineering feat indeed, and Jimmy's family had played a part in the whole project, which made their family legendary in Florida. But Jimmy had been left out of the hierarchy of the company, much as I had been up north. This realization gave me a new understanding of the man. We were probably more alike than I wanted to believe. I wanted to treat people better than he did, but it was just his tough, old-school way of operating—which I desperately hoped I would have to deal with again. I wanted back into Delta; it was my new home.

Jimmy told me that he would get back to me sometime that week. Waiting was tough. I felt foolish all over again, but all I could do was wait for the verdict. Would I work there again or be forced to go crawling on my knees to Uncle Pete asking for a job? The latter was not the option I was hoping for at all. My cousins were on that train, and I wanted no part of it. At least at Delta I had some autonomy. I could in time become my own man, I hoped.

After a couple of days Jimmy called me back. He said that he had a meeting with the whole company and put the decision to a vote as to whether I should be able to come back to work. They voted me back in. This was Jimmy's way of dealing with the favoritism issue. Instead of him letting me back in, the employees did. Nevertheless, I felt good that they voted the way they did. After all, it was their chance to throw me out. Maybe my trying to make friends and not be a jerk had been better received than I had thought. Life is a lot like that— either we are building good karma with people or not. It's like putting money in the bank and drawing it out when you need it. If you've built up good karma, there is something of substance to draw on; but if the karma you've built is bad, there's nothing there.

I began to make plans to prove my worth to the company and to myself. I was tired of my self-loathing and feeling sorry for myself. It was time to kick some ass and take charge of my life. It was time to forge a new self-image and put my past behind me, once and for all.

Chapter Eighteen

New Beginnings

I may have had a new sense of purpose, but I still had the same old boss. Jimmy didn't let up on me for even a second, always chiding me, getting under my skin, and never allowing me to feel comfortable. I had to endure because I knew the alternative. I was able to make friends with many of the crew members and foremen and thanked them for sticking by me in my predicament. It meant a lot to me and I told them so. My biggest problem at work was that I didn't have a real position, title, or specific job and that kept me on shifting ground. I had no "turf" to call my own. I would go out and measure jobs for estimating, take water jugs to the crews, set up construction signs for highway jobs, and just about anything to help out in the company, but something was always missing. I needed a larger sense of purpose, one that showed I had a sense of competence about the business of paving construction.

On October 5, 1978, Jillian Marie Azzarelli was brought into our little world. She was a seven-pound, six-ounce, bubbling, beautiful baby, and our lives were changed forever. Mary and I were ready for the responsibility and couldn't have been more thrilled about the prospects of our new family. I knew we had plenty of love to give to our next generation. Mary's mother made the trip down from Illinois to spend a week inaugurating Mary into motherhood and doing anything she could to help out. My life seemed to take on new meaning knowing that I had another mouth to feed. Words cannot explain the wide range of emotions exploding from deep within my spiritual consciousness, knowing that a new human being had been entirely entrusted to us. Another part of us was now on the earth. Jillian was truly a blessing from God.

The first few months were stressful for Mary, learning to be a mother, never sure of the right thing to do, and having no mother around to help out. It was somewhat frightening to see her go from her normal weight of 125 pounds down to about 110. She looked like skin and bones, but she loved it. Mary had never been a petite woman, but her five-foot, seven-inch frame always carried her weight gracefully and attractively. We were both learning to be parents together, and without much help from anyone else, it made the three of us that much closer. Jill learned to walk in only ten months. She always has been smart and a fast learner.

THE PAVING BUSINESS

There is quite a bit of daily planning in the paving business. We had two paving crews, and in order for everything to go well on a project, it had to be thought out yesterday: equipment had to get moved to the site, trucks had to be lined up in advance, and often the job to be done was not ready to be paved. If the paving equipment was moved to the site and some part of the job was not ready to have pavement laid on it, it could waste part of a day or the whole day all because of poor communication between the base crew and the paving crew. The base is the "ground" that the asphalt is laid upon, much as the earth is what sod is laid on. If the ground is level and graded properly, it is ready for the sod. Then the yard drains properly and looks uniform. Similarly, with asphalt, the pavement being laid needs to have a solid base below it that drains correctly and must support the weight of cars and large trucks over a long period of time. If the base is unstable, the asphalt will not hold up. The base in Florida is generally made up of limestone and installed about six inches deep. It takes great skill and expertise to grade a road or parking lot to professional specifications and make it acceptable for asphalt. Base crew foremen often will try to dupe the paving crew into doing a job before it is ready just to try to make their work easier.

Jimmy was doing the scheduling from his office, fielding the requests for jobs to be paved and setting up the advance work. However, he would not go to the sites. He preferred to work by phone and bark out the orders from his office. The foremen would often gripe to me about all the mistakes that were being made because Jimmy physically did not go out to the sites and inspect them with the base crew foreman. Mistakes can have a cumulative effect; an error that occurs today affects the whole schedule for the week and leads to upset customers who are waiting for their jobs to get paved.

This is when I saw my golden opportunity. I went to Jimmy one day in his office to discuss the situation. It took all the courage I could to tell him that many of these jobs were not ready, some of the equipment being moved were the wrong pieces going to projects, and often the wrong crew was placed on the wrong job. This was costing the company money. I told him he needed a field superintendent, one to coordinate all the operations on a daily basis. He asked, "Who do you have in mind?" I replied, "Me."

This was a chance to show assertiveness to Jimmy and show myself and the world that I could do it, whatever "it" was. I sought a chance to prove I could be of value in a company other than physically laboring, using my hands and trading time for money. If this worked, I could use my mind and abilities to plan, coordinate, and facilitate operations. I was both frightened and excited about the prospect of being free to use my experience and imagination—"working" the crews, making the business run with a fresh approach.

Jimmy promptly turned me down. He told me that I lacked both knowledge and experience and that no one would listen to me, since I was an Azzarelli. I lightly argued with him, knowing that his answer was final for now and that I would have to continue on the free-floating journey I was on at the time in the company. I tried to console myself that I was at least beginning to get a handle on estimating asphalt jobs and instituting traffic control plans with the Department of Transportation projects, which was a requirement with each job. At least I was learning many of the important facets of the asphalt business.

Then I disappeared. We had an ongoing, countywide street resurfacing program that required us to dig out driveways and install an asphalt base before the final surface could be installed. We had only two asphalt lay-down crews and no crew to dig out the dirt for these driveways and install the asphalt. I took it upon myself to do the job with only one other man to help. We were "gone" for about two weeks, not telling anyone what we were doing or where we were working. The truth is that I don't think anyone really cared or noticed that we were gone. I loved the fact that I could just go out without supervision, knowing that we were doing a nasty, tough but necessary task. Without getting that asphalt base installed, the crews of eight to ten men would have had to stop their moneymaking operations to perform this labor-intensive work.

After about two weeks, Jimmy must have been dying to know where I was. Finally, his blue Mercury Marquis pulled up to my job site. He rolled down the window and asked, "What are you doing?" I promptly responded, "Someone has to get this base in before we paved these roads, so I decided to go ahead and take care of it." Jimmy was speechless for the first time since I met him and probably surprised at my ambitiousness in undertaking a project that he had forgotten needed to be done. I had trumped him. A sense of satisfaction surged through me, as if my actions spoke much louder than the words I spewed in his office about a month earlier. At that time I remembered the Dale Carnegie class instructor telling me that in order to be enthusiastic, I had to act. So that's what I had done: I took action, backing up my claim that I deserved that job of superintendent over the crews.

I went about my business for about another week. There must have been seventy to eighty driveways yet to finish when the date for our monthly safety meeting arrived. Jimmy gave his usual speech about staying safe and looking out for each other. Then he reluctantly added, "We're going to let Jim here get the crews what you need. His daddy wanted me to make something out of him, so this is his chance." That certainly wasn't the way I wanted him to say it, but it was his back-handed way of saying that I was now in charge of all field operations in the company. I was floored, and all eyes were on me. I was thrilled and quite proud that I had conquered the hill—Jimmy Conner. I had finally gained his respect. I realized then that only one thing, hard work, got his attention. All the other rhetoric was just that, a bunch of crap that he didn't care about. He proved the old adage that "what you are speaks so loud that I can't hear what you're saying." I received a different vehicle to drive, which is a big status symbol in the hierarchy of a company, and was given the reins of running the field operations of Delta Asphalt, the job I had coveted since I had begun working there in February 1978.

Now it was time to produce. Achieving a job goal is only part of the excitement. It takes doing that job well to fully attain the thrill of accomplishment. I felt that sense of achievement and satisfaction of moving up the ladder of success, but I had a lot of anxiety about how the job was going to work out. I never felt comfortable working for Jimmy. And I was worried that, now that I had earned the promotion, he would only turn the screws harder on me. And he did. Much harder.

The Downside of Moving Up

The stress of planning the company's locations each day was large, but I knew I could do it. It required adjusting on the fly, changing directions like a flag in a thunderstorm. And I felt as if I were in a storm all the time, but I discovered that I really liked that feeling. I was learning to thrive under pressure. Each day I would drive a couple of hundred miles, looking at job sites and talking to construction people. These were the kind of guys I had grown up around, rough and tumble Marlboro-smoking types who enjoyed a beer or two after work. I felt like I had found my niche; this was me and I could handle the job. The downside was that Jimmy would pull me into his office and chew my backside out on a weekly basis, whether I needed it or not. I guess it was his way of letting me never feel too good about myself or my position in the company. I don't think Jimmy ever felt too good about himself or his position either. In any event, it was not fun to get berated in the boss's office, especially because he always hammered on the idea that no one around there respected me.

As time went on our relationship did improve somewhat. We golfed together occasionally during the week, which took some of the pressure off me for a few hours. But even playing golf with Jimmy was a bit stressful. I don't think he ever enjoyed anything. He just seemed like a tortured soul living in a lonely world.

At work, though, I was getting efficient at running the field operations. I had weekly meetings with the two crews to set up projects for the week and then contacted them as needed to make changes throughout the week. I discovered that the only constant in the paving business is change. As time wore on, I realized that this was true not only in my work but also in the larger scope of my life as well.

Real Estate and the American Dream

By 1979, I realized I needed to do more than my job if I was going to make any real money. I attended a real estate seminar created by Dr. Albert Lowry. The instructor explained that the only good investment in America was real estate, and he recommended that we put every spare dime we had into investment properties. I knew that working construction for others would never make me much real money, so I figured, *What the heck? Let's go for it.* I walked out of that seminar, and within a month I owned a duplex rental property in Tampa. It was a rundown black-and-white frame building on the south side of town, an area I thought would improve greatly over the next several years. I had it painted inside and out, laid fresh sod, and rented both apartments for $275 each per month. The property cost $35,000, and after the fix-ups it appraised for $60,000. I thought I had found the magic formula to wealth, so I refinanced the property and quickly bought another rental house, a two-bedroom with a rear apartment for $68,000. I didn't do any work to the house but had at least a break-even cash flow between the two properties during the winter months when people would flock to Florida. In the summer, people always moved out, leaving me with negative cash flows and scarce renters in the market. This did not deter me, however, and in September 1980, I bought another rental house just a few blocks from the other one.

I was on a roll, feeling the drive toward what I thought was surefire wealth and prosperity. In retrospect, I jumped a little too soon in buying that third one, as cash began to get very tight. The interest rates were 16 percent on the first house, 13 percent on the second, and 13 percent on the third. In spite of this, I became fixated with the idea of owning ten properties. I decided that nothing was going to stop me from getting rich.

Why is real estate such a large part of the American dream? I think it goes back to the land-grab days of the west, when so many people had the vision of moving out west and owning a piece of America. Just having title to a piece of ground in this country somehow validates us and includes us in what is great about this nation. The idea that no one can take it away from you is an enticing slice of the independent spirit of our forefathers. Nanu always said, "They aren't making any more land," so in other words, "Get yours while you can." I was out to get my name on as many deeds as possible in a short amount of time.

In order to make the monthly payments and hang onto the rental properties, I had to keep them occupied with paying tenants. I had my share of bad tenants in those early years. At that time, Tampa was like a wild frontier, where people would come and go like a whirlwind and often not pay their rent on time. This forced me to make several trips to the south end of town only to come up empty-handed. I began to get frustrated and would air my dirty laundry to Mary, who just didn't want to hear it. After all, she figured, I made these deals so now I just had to handle it. But I wasn't handling it well. Just as I would get the monthly mortgages paid, some problem would pop up at one of the properties and it would set me back hundreds of dollars. My blood would boil over, and she would fume at me about my attitude toward it all. Mary would say, "Why don't you just sell them all?" She had a good point. But I wanted to hang on to make good on my dream of being a real estate tycoon. Unfortunately, it was taking a toll on my marriage. When money would get tight and I had to deal with all of the property issues, I got increasingly moody. It wasn't good for our relationship, and it wasn't good for me.

Chapter Nineteen

Challenging Authority

In early 1981, we found out that Mary was again pregnant and due sometime in early September. We always knew that we wanted more than one child, and Jill was going to be three years old in October, so the time was right.

My job at Delta was going about as well as I could have expected. I had taken much of the field operation hassles away from Jimmy, and our relationship was about as good as it would get. He took me on a few asphalt paving conventions, in-state venues where a few meetings and much golf was on the menu, so I felt that I had some respect from him. Also, Jimmy had recently gotten married, and his wife, Shirley, and Mary got along pretty well. So I figured this was Jimmy's mellowing out that I had hoped for. However, at the office I was still the target of all of his denigrating remarks and sarcasm. This was wearing thin with me, but I maintained my course the best I could and plugged away at my real estate management.

Jimmy loved to call me into his office and rail on me about how much money I was losing out there on the crew because he had computer records to back up the facts. It gave him pleasure to show me that I wasn't doing a good job and that he could do better. One day, when looking over the computer records, it dawned on me that all those so-called losing jobs were J. W. Conner jobs. In those projects, the asphalt prices quoted by J. W. Conner & Sons were designed to make them money and for Delta to *lose* money. I realized I had trumped him again and I pointed it out to him. I asked the obvious question: "Why do we always lose on *your* family's jobs?" He just gave me that faraway look and didn't answer the question. Without knowing it, I had unlocked the dirty little secret inside the kingdom. The Azzarelli family was one-third owner of the business, and when Pete Azzarelli called Delta to get prices on paving projects, Richard, the estimator, gave him the standard market prices. This meant that Azzarelli received the short end of the stick on all these jobs. Jimmy never again sat down with me to show me all the money I had "lost" the company. The jig was up and he knew it. I even brought up this discovery to Uncle Pete and Uncle Joe, but they seemed not to care. Their attitude was that it was J. W. Conner Jr.'s company to run, and that's the way it was, so don't worry about it.

I began to become disillusioned as to what I was accomplishing at Delta. Pete had always made me feel as though I would one day be the general manager there, but now I wasn't sure that I wanted to. After all, we as a family had very little to say in the business, so what would the future hold there for an Azzarelli? Maybe I could change all that, but maybe not.

Amy Katherine Azzarelli was born Labor Day, September 4, 1981. She was somewhat bigger than Jill, weighing in at eight pounds, ten ounces, and she was a dreamboat. In the delivery room, we had paid a few extra dollars to do the Leboyer method of birth, where the room is dimly lit and the baby is immediately handed to me and I immerse her into warm water in a small bathtub and massage her until she is calmed down. It seemed to work, as I held my precious little girl in my hands and poured water over her body and soothed her until the crying stopped. It was an experience I'll never forget, one that I wished we would have done for all the kids' births. Amy and I have always been close, and I wonder if that experience had something to do with it.

Mary's mother come down again for another week to help out, but after that she was on her own to handle two kids now instead of one. Mary was adept at handling the situation now, having met many other friends in the neighborhood who could help her deal with the day-to-day chores of rearing kids.

We felt strongly that it was important for her to be home with the kids as they grew up. But it was the 1980s now, and many of the other women in the neighborhood had careers and were helping to pay the bills. That was fine for them, but that wasn't the way we wanted to go about rearing the kids. Mary and I both felt that they needed their mother at home.

While Jimmy continued to give me grief about anything and everything, he delighted in the fact that he predicted the day Amy would be born. He said she should be called "Jaimey" instead of "Amy." That was about as lighthearted as he could get. On one occasion, at a preconstruction meeting with the Florida Department of Transportation, he brought a Bible into the meeting. He sat in complete silence through most of the meeting, but everyone knew he was up to something. Near the end of the meeting he made a statement: "If you think you can build a road by that DOT manual, then I challenge you to try to live strictly by this Bible, and I doubt very seriously that anyone in this room lives by the good book." Everyone looked at each other and thought, *That's Jimmy.* Another time when I was setting up some signs for a DOT project, Jimmy came over the radio asking me what I was doing. I told him I was moving the signs to the project managers' specifications. He said, "Who told you to do that?" I replied, "Floyd Cherry." (Floyd was standing by the truck.) Jimmy said, "You tell him he doesn't know what the hell he's talking about." Floyd looked at me as if I were now the enemy and, as one might expect, proceeded to give us all hell for Jimmy's arrogance.

I learned a lot from Jimmy those years. For one thing, he taught me how *not* to treat people, but he also taught me plenty about the asphalt business and what one can and cannot do with hot mix asphalt. One time we were on a large road project when the skies opened up and lightening started popping everywhere. We had to shut down the job and send eight loads of asphalt back to the plant. Usually, this is done because the asphalt mix will chill down, stiffen, and become unacceptable to the inspectors on the job. The Department of Transportation requires a minimum temperature of 285 degrees for the mix to be laid down. The inspectors assumed we would dump them and lose thousands of dollars. But it was summer, when the nights in Florida are quite warm. Jimmy had the truckers' park in the shop without telling a soul. The next morning, he sent those loads back out and we laid them all. I didn't know what he'd done until one of the drivers told me later even though Jimmy had sworn him to secrecy. The inspectors never knew what he'd done, but he saved the company thousands in lost revenue. I realized then that asphalt will stay hot many hours, even overnight.

New Ambitions

In 1982, I turned twenty-nine. Some people say that this is when men start looking at their life with a longer perspective. I began thinking I might want to look for another career or at least another gig. I was worn out from having to deal with Jimmy the last four years. It was like being in a permanent boot camp, with no end in sight.

Through my work I came to know Dave Creeley, who was part owner of Larkin Contracting, a Tampa subdivision contractor who would regularly subcontract asphalt work to Delta. I would have to inspect Dave's base jobs prior to our laying the asphalt down. Often I would have to point out the deficiencies in the base, which were affecting our "yield" on the jobs. If the base was too low, then more asphalt would be required to make up for the dips in the base. This would cost our company money and lead to more "ass chewings" by Jimmy. I was caught in the middle. Dave thought the large quantity of work his firm gave us should offset the loss of asphalt on his jobs. But the amount of asphalt we were losing on some of his jobs was significant, and the amount of "chew outs" I received was mounting. I had to prove to Dave that the way he was constructing his roads was flawed. I used string line stretched from the curb out to the crown of the road to show the deficiency in the base. This created a low area in the road itself, thus requiring more asphalt than was specified on the job. He reluctantly agreed and we settled on a per-ton price for the extra asphalt.

Dave was a young entrepreneur from Ruskin, Florida, a small, tomato-growing town about twenty-five miles south of Tampa. In his twenties he bought a few dump trucks and started hauling dirt for contractors in the Tampa area. He was a friendly guy with a boyish grin that made him easy to warm up to. Dave was a redneck at heart, always chewing tobacco and spitting in a cup. While this habit was quite nasty to me, I knew there was something about this guy that I liked. In the early 1980s, he teamed with Sam Simmons, a stout, no-nonsense guy also from the Ruskin area with a famous last name in those parts, and Pat Larkin, who had started Larkin Contracting in Tampa back in the late 1970s as a pipe contractor. Together, Pat and Sam forged the company Dolphin L&S Inc. (Larkin & Simmons), and in due time Sam talked Dave into merging his trucking company with theirs to create a three-way partnership. Dave's contribution of trucks to the company became South Bay Trucking, but he was still part owner of Dolphin L&S.

In getting to know those three principals, I got to see firsthand how a construction company worked on the inside. I was able to hang out with Dave for long periods of the day. If

Jimmy wanted to know where I was, I told him, "Dave Creeley and I are looking at his jobs." I was soaking in everything Dave said. It was exciting to be with an owner of a company and listen to his ideas and philosophies on dealing with employees, making money, and handling all of his responsibilities. He had a carefree attitude about money, never worrying too much about it. This was a whole new outlook that I'd never seen before, since no one in my family ever showed me the ropes on the inside. I'd always been on the outside of the business loop, the field work side, which I had learned plenty about in my thirteen-plus years with the Azzarelli-Delta companies. Dave and I would ride his jobs for hours, with him showing me what was going on here or there in the company. One day, we finally made our way back to their office and we sat in Sam Simmons's office shooting the breeze. I was complaining about working for Jimmy when Sam made a suggestion that would change my life forever.

Sam came from a family that owned copious amounts of land in the south part of Hillsborough County. There is a Simmons Road there, a Simmons Loop, and even an E.G. Simmons Park. His family members have been influential in politics in Tampa as well. They had extensive cattle operations dating back to the nineteenth century, and Sam was a big thinker. Sam was cut from the Jimmy Conner mode as far as being a tough guy, but he was much more likeable. If he liked you, it was great.

He had a big grin on his face when he asked me, "Why don't we start a paving company and you can get the hell away from Jimmy Conner?" That started my wheels turning in a big way. I told him I'd think about it and maybe we could have another meeting in a week or so. Sam said, "Great," and I started thinking about owning my own company for the first time in my life.

Then I remembered what the psychologist back in Illinois had told me about this possibility. Never did I dream that I would consider such a giant, bold move as stepping out on my own, away from the family business. It seemed so radical at the time, as none of my cousins had ever done such a thing. In fact, no one in the family had ever had the balls or the timing to make such a move. All of us were still holding onto the idea that our futures had been laid out for us with our fathers' business. The great Azzarelli dream was the ideal of continuing in the footsteps of Nanu and the second generation, trying to carry forward the Azzarelli name in Tampa and Kankakee. My move down to Florida and the subsequent employment at Delta made me feel as though I was barely working for the family anyway. I felt that way more so in light of what I had discovered about the Delta bidding practices and our family getting the short end of the stick. No one at Azzarelli ever seemed to care too much about Delta anyway, but I had gotten one heck of an education there.

I was approaching thirty, and I was coming to a crossroad in my life. The idea of being on my own frightened me considerably. It would be like setting sail out to sea on my own, with no secure income and having to fend for myself. I had two young children to think about, a wife not working, a monthly mortgage payment, and the added pressure of rental properties and all that goes with them. It was going to be a big decision, for sure. Nanu was willing to step off a ledge into the great unknown for a chance at his American dream. I knew that if I made this move it would significantly alter my destiny, just as Nanu's was altered. The fear of failure was great, but the idea of not having to work for Jimmy Conner anymore appealed to me.

At night I would toss and turn trying to get a handle on what this would mean and what would be the consequence of failure. What if I fell flat on my face and had to go back to Jimmy? I would once again be the laughingstock of the company, having come back with my tail between my legs. That scared me. What if Jimmy wouldn't take me back and I had to go to Uncle Pete and beg? That was a horrible thought too.

I also had to consider my fledgling real estate investments, which were precarious at best. Some months they broke even, but most of the time it felt like I was simply going broke with them.

Within a couple of weeks, Dave, Sam, and I met at their office. We talked about the possibility of my buying into South Bay Trucking, but Dave didn't like that idea because that company was more of a tax write-off than a moneymaker. This dismayed me, because I felt if I could get a piece of that company, I would be able to hitch my wagon to their success; they were making big money at the time, grossing between $25–30 million per year. This would virtually assure success for me. While I would have three partners in the company, at least I would be free from the strings of Delta and the family. Dave suggested the idea of the three of us starting our own company and letting me run it from ground zero. That seemed like a long, uphill climb.

I left that meeting somewhat discouraged at my prospects for starting a company because I wanted some assurances that we would have success. Man, did I have a lot to learn. It was the summer of 1983, and President Reagan was trying to sort out the mess Jimmy Carter had in his presidency, and I was trying to sort out my own mess in my properties. My mortgage payments were about $2,400 per month, and my income from the rental properties during those summer months stooped to about $1,600. My salary was about $3,000 per month, and I had about $1,500 in savings. It was a grim financial picture, so I decided to continue with my work at Delta for the time being.

One day I was driving my pickup and I heard this commercial about an upcoming seminar in Tampa. The ad went something like this: "Every day you have to get up in the morning, look yourself in the mirror, and honestly ask, am I completely happy with what I am doing in life, or am I just doing this for a paycheck and not being true to myself? If it is the latter, then you have an obligation to yourself to make a change." What stuck with me was the old idea that the clock was ticking on my life and that every day counted toward my ultimate destination. Was I living my American dream? Partly. I was happy with my family, but I was a long way from being fulfilled at work. Maybe it was time for a change. But I was fighting the pull of the weekly paycheck and how easy it had become to stay put and not risk too much. I had become pretty efficient at my work and expediting asphalt paving projects as a supervisor.

Still, the lure of being an entrepreneur was calling me as strong as ever.

CHAPTER TWENTY

Making My Break

For a while, I let the idea of having my own company slide. We had become quite busy at the paving company, working six days a week paving the Crosstown Expressway in Tampa and several other large projects. However, we were about to lose Dolphin L&S, Dave's company, as a client. They were giving us about $2 million per year in paving business. I had a phone conversation with Dave concerning an overrun of asphalt on a job. As noted, some of their jobs required extra thickness, so we had to charge them extra money. We sent them a bill for the extra tonnage, and Dave wanted a discount. I told him that my hands were tied and that Jimmy wasn't going to give it to them, so he wanted to talk to Jimmy. I handed the call to Jimmy and sat back and listened to the "conversation" between the two. It was like watching a nature show in which two rams lock horns with each other until one ram just gives in and gets beat. Jimmy didn't give in but I think he got beat, because from that day forward we would not pave again for Dolphin L&S. Dave pulled the plug on Delta, and I wondered what that might do to our relationship. Soon thereafter, I visited Dave at his office to revisit the idea of my own paving business.

Dave told me that what we ought to leave Sam Simmons out of the deal because he wasn't that interested. Dave could start me out with at least $25,000 worth of business with his company right away. That was enough for me. I was done turning this deal over in my mind, wishing and wondering about my big dream. It was time to make it happen. This was another window I decided to climb through—hopefully, it was a window of opportunity to a brighter future. I started checking out the cost of equipment and figuring estimates on expenses for the company. My juices started to flow at what I felt could be a profitable enterprise. The first big step was giving Jimmy my two-week notice.

It was mid-October 1983 when I went into Jimmy's office for our weekly meeting. He immediately started telling me how no one in the company respected me and that I wasn't performing my job up to task and I needed to improve. It was the same old browbeating I'd become accustomed to. But this time was going to be different. I sat there with great satisfaction, waiting for him to finish. When he was finally done, I looked at him and said, "If I'm doing such a poor job, then I'm giving you two weeks' notice now. I'm leaving the company."

I'd never thought those words would come out of my mouth. It was such a relief. All the years of working for the family flashed before my eyes. It was really over. My future was now in front of me and would be determined by … me. Jimmy's eyes changed completely, as if he were looking at a different person. Maybe he was—someone who had decided to go ahead and risk it all. At first he interrogated me about my plans, and I grudgingly told him I was going to dabble in real estate and maybe even paving. Of course, he told me that it would be difficult and I wouldn't make it. I listened to all that nonsense out of respect, but I would not be deterred one bit, not by him or anyone else. The funny thing is, after that day Jimmy and I became friends. I walked out of that office with a new sense of self-respect and the cautious optimism that I was on my way to great things.

I went over to the Azzarelli office, where my dad now had an office. He had moved to Tampa in 1983 to establish the building division of the company in Florida, but had only marginal success. I wanted to break the news to him. I even gave him a window to be a partner in my business, but he promptly rejected the idea. He thought it was risky and that some calamity could happen and he would lose his fortune in a lawsuit. I told him that was fine and I went on my way planning for opening my and Dave's company. I had two weeks left to work at Delta but my mind was on the future.

After the first week, Jimmy called me into his office. This time it was totally different. He told me take the next week off, since he knew I had to make a lot of plans. He would take care of paying me my final check. I said good-bye to him and all my co-workers, and everyone wished me luck. I walked out with tears in my eyes of happiness and complete relief, knowing I would probably never again have to work for Jimmy or any other family business.

That ended my first dream of becoming an executive for Delta or Azzarelli Construction Co., but I was fulfilling another dream of Nanu's, one of forging my own way and listening to that still, small voice telling me to be my own man, make my own decisions, and rely on my own instincts. Maybe this would be the new Azzarelli dream, one in which we, the third generation, start in a new direction independent of our fathers' aspirations for us.

In early November 1983, Precision Paving of Tampa was incorporated in the State of Florida. For the first time since I was about fifteen, I felt free from any kind of supervision or control by others. That was the last time I had really been a kid, experiencing life on my own terms without having to prove anything to anyone. I was now free to do my own thing, create my own future, and be myself. I was experiencing a catharsis of sorts, a venting of my cumulative frustrations and anxieties pent up from all those years of working for abusive and old-school bosses who cramped my style. I was of the Woodstock and rock 'n' roll generation, and we had a new way of doing business. I knew the value of the work ethic handed down by Nanu and my dad's generation. But I had seen how the previous generation operated, in that they told employees only about their faults and never gave any praise for acceptable work. I wanted to work under the auspices of the Golden Rule, where people are treated the way I wanted to be treated.

I was on the cusp of the American Dream, being independent and self-reliant, the fundamentals upon which our great nation was founded. Think about those early settlers in Jamestown, in search of the New World and freedom from religious persecution. They suffered unrelenting hardships just to forge that new society. How about the American Revolution, where George Washington sacrificed his livelihood to lead the patriot troops into battles? That had to seem utterly absurd—fighting an enemy that was far superior—but he pressed onward and ultimately to victory. Or consider Abraham Lincoln, probably the most unlikely president in history, having to endure a war that threatened the existence of our union. He held in mind one ideal—that we had to remain together at all costs—only to be assassinated after the conflict. President Franklin Roosevelt faced the worldwide threat of the Germans and Japanese and having to lead our country through maybe the most frightening time in our history. He succeeded but surrendered his health, dying while still in office. Then, of course, there's the great immigration from Europe that made this country what it is today.

What is the common thread in all of this? I believe it's selling out to the dream, throwing out someone else's idea of what your life should become and carving out your path. By selling out I mean a total commitment to conquer your greatest fears, especially the fear of failure. It's facing the fear that we won't add up to what we should, that we will fall short of expectations. Who decides what is considered success or failure anyway? The definition of success usually comes from somewhere other than from within ourselves. We get our signals from others, as if we have to somehow measure up to this world's standards and what they are selling us on TV. We so often listen to others' opinions and think too highly of them, especially politicians who are trying to "sell" us on their concept of what America is and what our dreams are or should be. Our defining spirit comes from deep within our beings and must be transformed into the old spirit of exploration, innovation, and willingness to risk it all once again, as our founders did centuries ago. We cannot afford to follow the materialistic ideas that have been sold to us over the span of our baby boomer generation. It's time to take stock of ourselves again as a nation and learn to thrive in the sense of true freedom once again. We have it in us, and it is part of our destiny—for us and the generations to come. It can only come from each one of us individually as we continue our search for the great American Dream.

Stepping into the Dream

I started Precision Paving in our master bedroom in Tampa at a rolltop desk. I hired one man I had known back at Delta because he was in search of his own dream. At the time Don Temple was working under Jimmy Conner and making $4 per hour as a truck driver. He asked for a raise of twenty-five cents per hour but was turned down. Jimmy offered him a ten-cent per hour raise. That translates into about $4 per week and even in 1983 that didn't amount to much. I hired Don for $6 per hour and the dream of being my right-hand man for a new and growing company. He was the right guy for the job; he was willing to go the extra mile and do what was necessary for a fledgling enterprise. He was handy with engine repair, which was paramount to me because I was not.

At first Don and just sat in my house drinking coffee, discussing plans for the future, and waiting for the phone to ring, or scouring the town with our business cards in hopes of finding work. Work did come, but not so easily. At least I had a partner who was in a construction company himself. Dave was able to throw us work doing prime coating on base jobs his company was working on. This was the premise I started the company with; it launched with some guaranteed work and not totally from scratch.

That first Christmas on my own was one of the best I'd had. Mary and I had two beautiful daughters. Money was tight, but who cared? I had finally declared my independence. I was on my own and loving it. I was ready for anything.

In early January 1984, we found out Mary was pregnant with our third child. I hoped it would be a boy. We were living the American Dream, raising a family and starting a business together. Mary was my secretary—officially, she still is—secretary and treasurer of the corporation. The great perk was that I got to sleep with her.

At the time Precision was in its infancy, I was still hanging onto the dream of getting rich in real estate. I still had my three rental properties, which were a drain on our finances and our marriage. I still complained a lot about all of the management headaches, and Mary was still fed up with my whining. We went to a Marriage Encounter weekend sponsored by the Catholic Church, and I discovered that owning these properties caused her sadness in our relationship. This was disconcerting to me. I began to realize it was time to start unloading the real estate and focus on our relationship and the paving business. It went against my grain to sell those houses, but our marriage was far more important than my dream of wealth in real estate.

I put all the properties up for sale. I knew that one day those properties would skyrocket in value, but now was not the time to worry about it. I wanted to have a great marriage and a successful new business. Within twelve to sixteen months, the real estate was sold except for the three-bedroom, one-bath home in North Tampa. I made about $28,000 in profit on the houses, but that barely made up for all the monthly losses I had incurred through vacancies and other expenses. I felt a burden had been lifted from me, and Mary and I could now focus on getting our paving company off the ground and keeping our relationship on happier ground.

Patience has never been one of my redeeming qualities (which Mary would readily attest to), but when you are responsible for everything in a business, it's probably not so bad to be a little impatient. I was in a hurry to make something happen. I wanted to make a splash in the contracting business. I never wanted to just settle for the work my partner could manage to send our way; I wanted some real jobs as soon as possible. The first break came when a large fiber optic company installed their cables through Ybor City. They had to dig up the streets along the railroad tracks, and that required patching at a ten-inch-deep level. Our company got the contract, which amounted to about $33,000. That was the largest sum I'd seen up to that time. After that success, other work followed.

I learned quickly that *urgency* is the buzzword for owning a business. I felt that there was never time to relax or take a break because I was always under the gun to make payroll, pay equipment payments, and handle employees. Finding good employees is the difference between success and failure. Don brought what seemed like an endless supply of relatives to work for Precision, and I didn't mind because almost all of them were good workers and showed up on time, which in Florida was tough to find. Up north we always relied on the unions to supply our company with quality help, but in Florida it was up to me to find workers. Other than paying my people a fair wage, I've always tried to treat them with respect, and I suppose at times this attitude has cost me.

Sometimes people take my kindness as a sign of weakness and take advantage of me by stealing from the company or not giving their best effort. My weakness may be that I want everyone to like working for me, but many have paid the price for thinking I'm too easygoing. I've learned to be tough when it's appropriate. Just as a parent must scold a child, an employer has to reprimand an employee or even fire one, and I've had to do both.

On September 28, 1984, Jay Michael Azzarelli was born to Mary and me. We finally got our Little Leaguer, for whom I had hoped and prayed. He was born during Tropical Storm Isador, during hurricane season, which lasts from June 1 to November 30 each year. Jay brought his own storm with him, as he was colicky and kept us up at night. The crying would last hours at a time, but he was worth it, of course. Our children now were three years apart, which seemed to be a good separation.

At the end of 1984, Precision Paving had been in business a full year and we had sales of $400,000, which impressed me. We netted $100,000. I started thinking that running a business wasn't as hard as everyone had told me it was going to be. My dark clouds loomed on the horizon, however.

CHAPTER TWENTY-ONE
Going Out on a Limb

It was very satisfying at the end of my first year to know that the company and I had done pretty well. It gave me confidence that I wouldn't have to go crawling back to Uncle Pete for a job. At that point, however, came the pressure to outdo myself for the next year. My partner's company was booming as the real estate engine in Tampa began to heat up and subdivision work exploded. Our prime-coat business picked up considerably that second year, and our sales increased by about 30 percent, to more than $500,000. Our profits were only about $120,000, but I had to take into consideration that I was making about $42,000 and my partner, Dave, was making about $21,000. This was the most money I'd ever made.

During that summer of 1985, Dave and I purchased a five-acre tract of land in southeast Tampa with a four thousand-square-foot building on the front part of the property. Dave put up the money for the down payment, and I supplied the pavement repairs on the parking lot. I arranged the loan from my bank, which gave us a monthly payment of $3,500. I managed to find a crane rental company to rent the property for $7,000 per month. We were making a profit of $3,500 each month, and I thought we'd hit the big time—and for a while we did. I opened a separate checking account, and by the end of the year we had about $25,000 in the account. I never dreamed it could get that good!

That year the Chicago Bears had their best season since 1963, going 15-1 and sweeping through the playoffs, beating up on the Giants and the Rams and shutting them both out in the process. One day, after playing golf with Dave, I mentioned the possibility of going to the Super Bowl in New Orleans. He didn't bat an eyelash. He said he would get the tickets if I would make travel arrangements. My brother Greg is one of the all-time great Bear fans, and I had to include him in this. He had already gone to both of the playoff games when I called him to ask him if he wanted to go with Dave and me to the big game. He thought I was joking at first, but then he realized that I do not joke about such big deals. I chartered a private jet to fly six of us, including Greg, Dave, Pat Larkin, Sam Simmons, and one Pat's business associates from Tampa to New Orleans on the day of the Super Bowl in January. We all went to the "Big Easy" for some serious partying and the Bears vs. Patriots. We rented a limousine, drove down Bourbon Street, went to the world-famous Brennan's Restaurant, went to the game, which the Bears won easily, and generally lived large for a day. Greg always remembered that day, and I loved being able to show him such a good time. It was just the type of event I had always dreamed about when I was living up north. Big things were going on in Tampa, and now I was able to take part in some of the festivities.

My accountant, Charlie Blake, had always told me that I would tire of having a partner, but I'd never taken him seriously. Dave always seemed as easygoing as I was. During 1986, however, he started seeing the success the company was having and wanted more, explaining that he wanted to make the same salary as I was, about $45,000. I felt that was too much because this was my livelihood. I was doing all the work and he was basically a silent partner. He did help out with what work he could dig up for us, but I still felt this was unreasonable. The seeds of discontent were brewing, and I started to see what Charlie had been talking about. By late 1986 I started entertaining how I could buy Dave out of the business. This meant I was considering entering uncharted waters. For the first time in my life, I was contemplating running a business by myself, with no partner for support. All through my life I had always leaned on someone else to be there financially. If I made this move, I would be on my own, independent of any outside interference, but also without the safety net of knowing someone was there if I failed. This was a frightening thought.

I decided it was best for me to go make Dave an offer to buy him out. It was tough to do because we'd always gotten along so well, but I knew it would be for the best in the long haul. I didn't have much cash, and I didn't want to have to make monthly payments because they would burden me with too much debt. Then a flash of brilliance hit me. I could let him have the property we'd purchased together. He had made the down payment, and it was making money each month. It had a lucrative option on it, one that when exercised would give him several hundred thousand dollars of profit, so it was a good deal for him and me. This was another one of those windows of opportunity I recognized and was able to take advantage of.

Dave took the deal. I figured over the next twenty or so years I would have paid Dave more than a million dollars in salary and bonuses, so it was good deal for me too. I was betting on myself, as I was now completely on my own for the rest of my life. I was willing to take this gamble because, after all, I was doing most of the selling, administration, and work supervision in Precision Paving.

However in late 1986, storm clouds were gathering—the likes of which I'd never seen and wished I would never see again.

Jim Azzarelli

FACING ADVERSITY

In 1985 we had purchased a small paving machine, one that could mostly pave parking lots, driveways, and golf cart paths. Late in 1986, a man named Cleveland Hill called me with a couple of projects to pave. He said they were quite large, and I thought this was my big chance to make it big in this business. It turned out that these jobs almost put me out of business. The first project was a large Baptist Church in Indian Rocks Beach, which required paving large roadways and using a sizeable quantity of asphalt. We were on that job for about four weeks, which is an extended period for a paving job. Not many of our jobs lasted more than a couple of days. After the first couple of weeks, Cleveland told me he had a check for me at his office. It turned out to be the big setup. After paving there a couple more weeks, Cleveland told me there was another paving project north of Tampa, a shopping center. Upon commencing the second project, I began to inquire about the money for the first job at the church. He made the usual excuse—that he had not been paid yet—and I thought everything would be all right. It wasn't. Cleveland stiffed me for about $57,000 on the first job and nailed me for another $55,000 on the second job at the shopping center. To make matters worse, my ex-partner, Dave Creeley, had tried to get me to do some paving for his company, but I told him we were too tied up with these larger projects, so he enlisted another company to do his work. I was set back more than $110,000 and lost one of my best customers, Dolphin L&S. I was about as down as I could get. I'd never experienced any serious adversity before in business, and I was now receiving more than my share.

Cleveland Hill was a flashy guy with several cars who claimed to be my ticket to the big time, but he was a mirage in the desert. Later I learned that he masqueraded as a minister and wound up doing time in the slammer for selling coke. That did not surprise me one bit. This was a hard lesson, and it caused me to go into debt to the tune of more than

$100,000. Luckily, I had a friend in the banking business, Mike Pupello, who helped me get the funds I needed to get through this very difficult time. When I was blindsided by this downturn, I turned to many motivational speakers, such as Zig Ziglar, Wayne Dyer, Jim Rohn, Anthony Robbins, Earl Nightingale, and Brian Tracy. I had the Nightingale-Conant catalogue and would send for many of the tapes to listen to in my car for inspiration.

The hard part of going through the bad times was finding the will to keep striving to make something positive happen. I had three young children at home and a wife counting on me, but the pull downward was getting a grip on me and I had to fight its negative force. I couldn't believe I had just bought out my partner at such a cost and now everything was crumbling like a house of cards. I kept wondering, *Why did I buy Dave out?* I had to fight the urge to look back at all the fun we had going to the Super Bowl and putting money in the bank. I kept borrowing more money and listening to my tapes, over and over again. I was looking for answers as my dream seemed to be coming to an end.

Somehow, I kept dredging through 1987, and then came the market crash in October. Could things get any worse? I managed to keep going, getting jobs as I could, keeping the crews together, and making the debt payments. In 1776 Thomas Paine wrote, "These are the times that try men's souls," and my soul was under its first real test—the test to see if I had the will or the courage to continue in my own business. It would have been easier to give up and run back to the family in utter defeat. I realized for the first time that, as an employee, you may be concerned how your employer is doing and whether you have a job tomorrow, but you don't have to take the company home at night with you. I began to understand how my dad had gotten ulcers through so many years of contracting. I did not get an ulcer, but anxiety and depression had a pretty good hold on me. I had met with an uncommon success in my first few years in business, and I was unprepared for this upheaval. This setback affected Precision Paving for years.

In 1988 we discovered Mary was pregnant again. It was one of the few joys I had during that year, knowing that we were going to fulfill my dream of having four children. On August 16, 1988, Andrew James Azzarelli was born. The whole family was overjoyed at having a newborn in our house. Jill was now almost twelve, Amy, eight, and Jay, five. The age difference was a nice separation for the siblings, as they all were old enough to enjoy Andrew as an infant.

I hired an attorney to seek the money due me, and it took plenty of time to get anywhere. It seemed that the system was on the side of the crook, Cleveland Hill. He got paid and made off with the cash, and no one at the general contractor's office at either job cared much to help me out. After two long years of battling through many meetings and summary judgments, I finally got paid some of the money owed. On the first project I was paid $28,000 out of $55,000, which only paid part of my asphalt bill. On the second job I was paid $40,000 out of the $55,000 owed, and much of that went to the asphalt bill for that job. We were scuffling at best, merely keeping our head above water. Each day was a struggle to stay afloat. Thanks to Mike Pupello and the Key Bank, we would survive until 1990. But as the new decade was ushered in, the economy was in a recession, so it wasn't the coming boom time for which I had hoped.

My prime-coating operation took a big hit when Dave's company decided to buy their own prime truck distributor. Some of my other customers in town did this as well, so I had to rely on the asphalt patching and paving parking lots to see the company through. The years 1990 and 1991 were not good in our town, as I'm sure it was for much of the rest of the country. In 1990 I was able to procure the Hillsborough County School contract, which breathed some life into the business. I knew public money was the best way to survive a downturn because the government always spends money no matter how pitifully the economy is doing. The big problem, as I saw it, was that the savings and loan crisis had undermined our whole money system. The failures of more than one thousand S&Ls in the 1980s cost the government about $125 billion and created a huge federal budget deficit, which caused a real estate downturn and severely affected the construction industry. I knew things were bad when almost any job we did generated fear over whether or not we'd be paid. At least the school board paid its bills during that time.

We limped through 1991, and I remember saying to a colleague of mine who sold asphalt, "It can't get any worse than this, I guess." Then he said he was pretty sure that 1992 was going to be worse. I didn't want to believe him, but he was right. In 1992 I felt as if we were hobbling on our last leg. Little work had been coming in, and the school board work went to another firm. I was desperate. By then I had no office staff, and the only phone I had at my ramshackle office was forwarded to my car cell phone, which rarely rang.

I managed to get a large shopping center resurfacing job, which took at least six weeks. I employed only four people besides myself in an effort to keep my expenses down. Then, early in '92, I learned that Don Temple, my first employee, was running his stock car on my auto parts account. He had free access to it because I counted on him to repair the equipment as necessary. I had noticed the bills were quite high at the time, and I would question him about it, but he would always deny any wrongdoing. Then one day a parts store owner alerted me to the fact that he attempted to do it at his store, and Don's fate was sealed. On the Monday morning after my discovery, I fired Don without any reservations. It wasn't tough to do because Don had been slacking off, thinking he didn't have to work hard anymore because he had worked himself into a position of authority. How wrong he was! I was physically working harder than ever just to keep the company moving, and he thought he could take it easy.

In 1993 I bought a small road grader and hoped to expand the business into the grading and site development aspect of construction. I knew enough about it because I'd been around it during my years at Delta, plus I'd spent a lot of time at Precision dealing with base crews as part of our lay-down operation. It was the first time in about seven years I had even thought about expanding the business, and it was an aggressive move. I also bought a two-yard loader and sought out site development jobs such as Taco Bell, churches, and Walden Bookstore. We had marginal success that year, but as 1994 dawned I made a bold move. I hired a real estimator to handle my bidding for site projects. He wanted $700 per week, at which I almost gagged. I was making only about $45,000 a year myself, but I knew I had to have this guy. So I took a big leap of faith and hired Buddy Brooks. It was a good move. I also hired a front desk girl with modest experience, but at least I had someone there to answer the phones.

Buddy Brooks was a fifty-seven-year-old construction esti-mator with at least thirty-five years experience in the busi-ness. He was as honest a man as I'd ever met, and I needed that virtue at this point of my career. He had some contacts who helped us get a better foothold in the site construction business in Tampa, and I was thrilled to have a right-hand man who would stand behind the company and serve as my confidant. I had the audiotapes "The Power of Positive Thinking," by Norman Vincent Peale, and Buddy asked if he could borrow them. I never got them back, but I'm sure they changed his life. He had been married five times for various reasons but settled down after we worked together. I'm not sure if I'd influenced him or if Reverend Peale did, but he be-came an elder in his church and a dedicated family man. He died on September 24, 2006, after working with me for the better part of twelve years, and I miss him dearly. He taught me so much about the site work industry.

After Buddy came in as my main estimator, our business took off and our sales went to more than $2 million per year for the first time. Two of Don Temple's sons were still with me in the paving division, and we developed two site crews who kept steadily busy. My office had been in a shack at the Azzarelli Construction compound, and it was completely dreadful. At one point during a rainstorm the ceiling started leaking and the computers got wet. I decided it was time for a change.

In 1987 I had bought a 2,500-square-foot building on a twenty thousand-square-foot lot in east Tampa. I bought it to house the equipment and do maintenance and repairs there. Now, I had the confidence to construct some offices in that building and move out there. For the first time in the history of Precision Paving, all of the operation would be under one roof. In 1995–1997, with Buddy on board, the site work division helped the company expand to more than $3.5 million in sales. I was excited that we had made such great strides in the construction world, and I wanted more—a lot more. The only struggle we encountered during those years was the constant theft by employees taking liberties on me because of my lack of organizational skills. Many of the guys had Home Depot credit cards, given by the company, and they used them freely for their own needs. I did not know what was going on. My front desk girl, Robin, had no idea either, but it would show up on the bottom line. We were constantly losing money, always running at a deficit. Although our sales were doing well, the monthly statements didn't look like it. At the end of the years 1998, 1999, and 2000, we showed losses, and I could never get a comfort level about where we were headed. Little did I know it, but even bigger storm clouds were headed our way.

Chapter Twenty-Two
The Dark Night of the Soul

In June 2001, I took my family on a trip to the Bahaman Islands. It was one of the few relaxing vacations we had ever taken because most of our trips were to Illinois to visit family. Upon my return, Robin took me into my office and revealed to me that we were behind in our asphalt bills to the tune of $200,000. She had been afraid to tell me the bad news and hadn't wanted to ruin my vacation, so she waited until I returned. I was dumbfounded and couldn't believe our predicament. Delta Asphalt not only was my ex-employer, but also my first creditor, selling me all the asphalt needed in my business. Owing them that much cash was embarrassing and heavily weighed upon my shoulders. I started to wonder if there were other bills that were past due. There were more, much more.

On September 11, two hijacked jets flew into the World Trade Center, destroying the buildings and killing almost 2,800 people. As I watched in horror with the rest of the country as our largest city was attacked, I couldn't help feeling that my own world was crashing down as well. Little did I know then that my business was headed for the biggest decline ever as the fallout from the terrorist attacks would have far-reaching consequences for me and the nation. The next winter my insurance tripled, and I decided to drop my carrier because he was gouging me. It cost me plenty: I had to pay $27,000 to start with a new insurance company, but it was worth it because I wanted to prove a point to my old agent. I had to pay that on a Friday, payroll day, so it was painful having to scrape together the cash.

During the Thanksgiving break my secretary quit and I decided to pay her desk a visit. Looking below her lap drawer under the desk, I noticed a pile of unopened envelopes. She had a stack of bills that were at least 90–120 days past due. My heart sunk as I checked out each of the bills. She had not been paying many of our creditors for some time. I knew we were in big trouble. In all, we owed out about $600,000 as opposed to $300,000 in receivables. I began to doubt that we would survive this turn of events. I began immediately to call these creditors and explain my situation and pledged to pay everyone in due time if they could just be patient with me. Most of the credit managers understood, but soon I began receiving legal notices from attorneys. I was being sued by no less than five creditors. I had never been sued in nineteen years of the business. I was nervous and anxious about our future. Right after Thanksgiving, I hired a new office manager, Angi Knowles, who immediately began to wonder what she got herself into by coming to work for Precision Paving.

I called the attorneys representing my creditors and tried to cut deals with them. Many of them discounted their amounts owed. I called the other creditors and set up payment plans, offering $100–$300 per month in payments. In the meantime, I visited a bankruptcy lawyer. We talked about the possibility of filing Chapter 11, but she said that would be complicated and time-consuming. She described having to go downtown and talk to a judge and let him decide who I could or not pay each day. It sounded like a real hassle, but I felt as if I were running out of money and time. The other option she described was Chapter 13, where I would shut down this business, stiff everyone I owed, and start a new business. I told her thanks but no thanks. I would not consider that option because so many people were willing to be patient with me. She just smiled and said, "We'll see you back here later," and I replied, "Maybe so and maybe not."

I felt as if I were in a pool of quicksand. I didn't want to get up in the morning and go to work. I was living in fear, wondering when the next lawsuit notice would come to the office or to my house. I wanted to run as far away as possible. I felt the fight-or-flight response weighing on me like never before. The world seemed like a big, cruel place with nowhere to run or hide. All my weaknesses were exposed, and I felt small and embarrassed at my own plight.

The next spring I got my wish about doing larger site projects. I contracted to do a big grocery store-shopping center complex, and I thought this would be my ticket out of my financial mess. The job went okay for a while, but then costs got out of control and my asphalt paving crew quit in the middle of the job. I'd never had an entire crew quit all at once, and I was devastated. I remembered my dad's plight back at the Tampa Shipyard project and how desperate he had become. I was now in that pit myself. We tried to sub-contract paving work, but there wasn't enough profit to cover overhead and our other monthly payments. I tried to remember all I had learned on those motivational tapes and my Dale Carnegie classes. No matter how much positive thinking I tried to do, I couldn't get past this feeling of sinking into oblivion. After nearly twenty years of owning a company, it was supposed to get easier, but it wasn't the case.

In August 2002, Mary went to Kankakee for a wedding, and I stayed back in Tampa, trying to work through the mess. Lying in bed one night, I was contemplating my plight, and I began to wonder what it would be like if I just wasn't around anymore. I thought that ending my life would be easy to do—just grab a few beers, go out to the car, start it, and go to sleep. I couldn't believe my own thoughts! But it was an option—not a very good one, to be sure—but it was a way out of an ugly situation, one where I had failed miserably, not performing up to my own or anyone's standards. I had sunk to a new low. I got out of bed sleepless, desperate, and frightened at what I was thinking about. Could I really do it? No … yes … no. Then I remembered reading or hearing about desperate people who turned to the Bible. They just opened it and read a verse, looking for inspiration. I got the Bible, said a prayer, and opened it.

I read where the Lord has every hair on our head counted and he feeds the sparrows of the field, so won't he give us all that much more if we believe in him? I had not been that much of a Bible reader up until that time. I cried at the thought of the possibility of doing myself in. I thought about my two boys upstairs and what it would be like for them to find their dad in the car the next morning. I went back to bed and fell asleep. The next morning I made a vow to start reading the Word each morning. I realized that maybe I was undergoing the test, the test we are all put under. I started to count my blessings and realized that maybe it was more than just money that created true success. I had been so fortunate to have a great wife, four healthy children, and a great mother, father, and extended family. I had all the material things I'd ever needed, so what was so bad? In the Bible God told various prophets to get up and go take care of business, and that is what I felt was going on here. I wasn't hearing any voices, but I knew it was time to get a hold of this adversity and move forward.

I found a new perspective on the business and went about doing the best I could each day, paying off my bills and thanking God for getting me through my "dark night of the soul." I wasn't anywhere near pulling out of my tailspin, but I knew it had to start somewhere—and that was deep within me. My spirit had to lift up and soar again, rising above the fray.

I started to believe there would be some light at the end of my long, dark tunnel of recession and depression.

Maybe once again, just like during the Vietnam War, I was going through what much of the rest of the country was going through right after 9/11. Much of the nation was adversely affected due to the downward spiral of the insurance industry. Businesses were in a funk due to the general malaise everyone experienced at the nation's vulnerability exposed in being attacked at the heart of our nation's largest city and the capital of our country.

I thought about Smitty living in Washington, D.C., and decided to call him to see if everything was okay. He has a son, Danny who went to school at that time near the capital building. We both commiserated at what had happened to our country over the last thirty years, since our college days. We talked about the chill in the air that the nation was experiencing, what was happening to us as a people, and where we were headed.

LIFE GOES ON

In January 2003, the Tampa Bay Buccaneers ended their twenty-six years of futility by winning the Super Bowl in San Diego. I was there with a friend and was delighted at not only the outcome but that I had been there to see it. The Bucs had come a log way, and so had Precision Paving. The sun shined on the Tampa Bay area that spring as we won the big game and the economy showed signs of improvement. I was happy for our city and proud that I had endured the worst drama of my life as a businessman.

On March 20, U.S. and British troops invaded Iraq in a move designed to oust Saddam Hussein and begin to avenge the attacks of 9/11. It seemed as if President Bush was as sick of being kicked around as I was during my great fall in business. That spring I hired my brother Rick as an estimator and confidante to help me come out of the doldrums. I hired a new and productive paving crew, and things started to turn around gradually. We were able to procure a couple of profitable jobs, and by the end of 2003 the company showed a small profit for the first time in six years. It had been a long drought, but a combination of hard work, new employees, and a renewed faith in God saw me through the greatest depression of my life.

My woes weren't over, however. On June 21, 2004, Rick said our usual prayer before breakfast, and we began eating when Rick's cell phone beeped. It was a call from our truck driver, Charlie Jackson. He said, "I just killed a man." He was about five miles from where we were eating, and we drove up to the spot immediately. I pulled up where the truck was stationed out on the road and saw a corpse lying on the highway.

It was a sight I had never seen, and it shook me to my bones. The Florida Department of Transportation was on the scene with about eight troopers, and the road was barricaded off. Charlie had been our main dump truck driver for about eight years and had never received a ticket. A motorcyclist had pulled out in front of the truck, and Charlie never had a chance to stop. He dragged the guy about 150 feet to his death. The truck was impounded but released the next day. The State of Florida fined Precision Paving $5,000 for not complying with all the new rules we had failed to enforce for truck drivers, such as keeping accurate paper records of our vehicles' condition on a daily basis. More damaging, however, was the toll it took poor Charlie. He had to endure his own dark night of the soul, not being able to sleep, having flashbacks of seeing that motorcycle driver's head go down in front of his truck. He would never drive a large dump truck for us again.

Just as we started our rise from the ashes, we were dealt another setback. This fatality was more of a psychological blow; in a strange way, I felt responsible, even though it wasn't our fault. Seeing the body on the pavement etched an impression in my mind that I couldn't let go of for a while. As the years have gone by, I have learned to put adverse conditions on a scale of one to ten. Being stiffed for large amounts of money in 1986 was about an eight. The firing of my first employee for stealing was a seven. The poor economy of 1991–1992 was a seven. My depression of 2001–2002 was a nine, but the fatality on the highway a ten. This is my way of trying to gain perspective on all the twists that owning a business can throw at a person. Just when I get over one bad deal, another one pops up. I used to lose it when equipment would break down or I would hear a bad report about an employee. Now I just see those small instances as routine occurrences. In 2005, we had no less than three accidents involving our trucks and were sued twice, losing both cases. Insurance has continued to rise due to these losses. Regardless, I feel I must press forward at all cost.

In May 2007, my son Jay graduated from the University of Florida, as both Jill and Amy had done previously. Jay soon expressed an interest in working in the business and since has become somewhat of my right-hand man. Another part of my American Dream had fallen into place, perhaps. Jay was conceived only a month or so after I started the business, and now he is the general manager and hopefully will one day take over for me. Andrew, my youngest son, has a world of possibilities before him. It seems we have all come full circle.

Nanu's dream was to find a better life for his family and himself, and he did so. He is gone, but his dream lives on in his two remaining sons, thirty grandchildren, and more than seventy great-grandchildren. It was a dream born of hard work and sacrifices, by him, Nana, and the six kids all willing—and sometimes not so willing—to pitch in to help the cause. That's the point: whether or not they wanted to do the work, there was no questioning the common purpose that was behind the effort of that family. It's probably where our baby boom generation took a detour in our own quest for the American Dream. We decided what we wanted or didn't want to do, and we became rebellious in our own right. That can be positive sometimes, but it can also be destructive, and we've probably had much of the former infect us as a generation. In deviating from our fathers' and grandfather's ways, we upset the balance of the American experience and pushed it past the point where rebellion was a positive force within our ranks. It made us all want to do our own thing, and that created disharmony in the union. Just as Nanu was the unifying force within my father's company, upon his death, the family business split up and that eventually led to its demise. After almost forty years in Tampa, the business closed its doors. It was over for them. The business in Kankakee continued to operate until 2000, when it was sold to another construction company.

In many ways, it's the same way with America. Our country has grown from respecting authority enough to do whatever we were told for the common good, to becoming rebels without a cause, not wanting to be governed and cynical toward anyone with common sense and a greater vision for America. We have now come to question authority as we were told to do so back in the 1960s, even when that authority is looking out for our own good. We don't believe anyone can know what is best for us—we only want what feels good or sounds good today. We want our ears massaged and to delay at all cost any pain that surely will come with this type of attitude. It's like not disciplining your kids because it's easier not to do so and then waiting for the eventual outcome—they become brats! We must all begin to take ownership of our country, realizing that we are passing on a legacy and an ideal to the next generations and the freedom that comes with it. That's the reason it was founded and why Nanu came here in the first place.

The Great American Dream

America is the great melting pot for the world. Everyone here is trying to latch on to something that is important to them individually, something they can attain. It is as personal and individual as the DNA that makes up each person around the globe. We call it the American Dream because it is on this land, but the dream is universal in that everyone wants the same thing—freedom to express themselves, whether in speech, action, or making an extra buck for their family. The dream is just more attainable in America because of the efforts of many people who felt it was important for freedom to exist. Everyone around the world wants the same thing, but so many face roadblocks. We've become, as Pink Floyd said, "comfortably numb" to the idea that we *do* have opportunities to do as we please.

Maybe some of us want to get rich, and that's okay, but there's a price to pay for that too. Not everybody is out for the same thing. I've worked at Metropolitan Ministries in Tampa, where the homeless gather daily, and many of them are comfortable living in the streets. They get their daily bread and move on. I've often thought maybe they just don't want all the hassles of the daily grind that I have to deal with. It's what they are comfortable with, and we who are "more fortunate" are willing to give of our surplus to help sustain them. That giving helps us to feel okay as well. It's not that one is a better person than the other; it's that everyone has different aspirations and desires.

I aspired to get rich, but I soon found all the pitfalls, failures, and the grind I was put through before I was my own boss. Then I traded bosses for clients who didn't want to pay or were unreasonable. For the most part, I just played the cards that were dealt and made the best of it. It never was easy and it still isn't. A lot of us attain the wealth we desire and then find that money isn't all there is to being happy. Working so hard often involves sacrifices that include giving up quality time with the family, which subsequently leads to divorce— very prevalent in the baby boom generation. Many of us sacrifice our health to obtain wealth, and then spend all of our money to try to regain our health. We are so focused on what makes us happy that often those we love the most become our sacrificial lambs—all in the name of the American Dream.

This is the part of the dream that has become a nightmare for our generation, the loss of the basic, most sacred part of society—the nuclear family, which has always been the backbone of America. It's what we boomers remember the most growing up: the tough World War II vet dad, driving the sedan with mom, and a sibling or two whom we couldn't stand growing up but now have become close to. Maybe the Norman Rockwell days are gone, but the child within us longs for them all the more as we move father and farther away from them. The old America longs to make a return trip back, and it can; it's just going to take some effort from each one of us in our own way. We have to dig down to our roots as a people and see what's most important to us. We have to see that the real America is more than the latest high-tech gadget or designer jeans. We must find that piece of America that is deep inside of our soul, the America that survived the

Revolutionary War, the Civil War, World War I, World War II, Vietnam, and now the Iraq War.

My butt was on the line worrying about going to Vietnam. Now all of our butts are on the line, but we don't want to face the music. We'd rather be politically correct with the rest of the world or be apathetic about world politics. With that kind of an attitude, we can be led in any direction the wind blows. To a large degree, that is what's happening today. As much of the media says today, we are a divided country, and a house divided cannot stand. That's what tore us apart during the Civil War and took so much bloodshed and time to repair. Sometimes it seems we're divided in politics with more hatred and bitterness than ever before, but I don't think we are as far apart as network TV and cable news channels want us to believe. Just look at what happens after a disaster: Americans are always right there to lend a hand or give cash to those in need after these events. We willingly send our money overseas to help tsunami survivors or other victims of nature's calamities. These instances prove that the heart of America is solid gold and that this country can and will stand for many generations to come.

It's a sad fact of life that bad news sells. If we can just keep this in mind, we can keep the heart of America pure with the intent to remain united while the media and the rest of the world try to tear us apart. We can and somehow will do this because deep inside of us is a love that the Almighty placed there. That's the only real thing we can hang our hats on. That is what will keep us united through terrorist attacks and the devastation of the family. We face so many tough issues today we must find a solid ground that has stood the test of time . It's what made me turn to the Bible in my time of my greatest distress, a book that has withstood two thousand years of upheaval.

My faith is my rock among the constant storms of my life. My family has become my American dream because I know they are who I've been working for all these years. We all have to have a reason to overcome struggle and strife, to do those things which are hard. It would have been easy for me to quit when it got difficult, but the reason I kept going was stronger than the pull of failure (and it didn't hurt having a great wife pushing me to get off my butt).

In these times of national struggle, we must get an old-time American perspective on keeping our union strong through loving each other and looking in the same direction, much as the founding fathers did. They had their differences, but they had a common vision, a purpose, a reason to stand united against Great Britain and its tyrannical form of government. We must now find that same bond. I believe it's the Great American Dream, and it will prevail and hold us together for the long haul. It's still alive in you and me.

Five of the original Azzarelli siblings are now deceased. I am lucky to still have my father, Sam, who just turned eighty-seven and is doing great. Bart Azzarelli, the great utility mastermind, died one day after his ninetieth birthday in October 2008. My daughter, Jill and son-in-law Trey have given us Caroline Elizabeth, our first grand child in November of '07. Having grandkids is everything I've heard and even more. I didn't expect to be this giddy about it, but it blindsided me, and my own children can't believe how excited I get when I see her little face. Life seems to have come full circle. The ride still can get rough at times, but I am learning how to handle the bumps a little better. As Mary says, "It's all in your attitude," and it's taken me more than thirty years hearing that to finally have it sink in.